What the Cat Dragged In

Poetry, Stories and Essays.

Lynda Stephenson

outskirts press

What the Cat Dragged In
All Rights Reserved.
Copyright © 2019 Lynda Stephenson
v3.0

This is a work of fiction. Names, characters, businesses, places, events, locales, and incidents are either the products of the author's imagination or used in a fictitious manner. Any resemblance to actual persons, living or dead, or actual events is purely coincidental.

The opinions expressed in this manuscript are solely the opinions of the author and do not represent the opinions or thoughts of the publisher. The author has represented and warranted full ownership and/or legal right to publish all the materials in this book.

This book may not be reproduced, transmitted, or stored in whole or in part by any means, including graphic, electronic, or mechanical without the express written consent of the publisher except in the case of brief quotations embodied in critical articles and reviews.

Outskirts Press, Inc.
http://www.outskirtspress.com

Paperback ISBN: 978-1-9772-1401-0

Library of Congress Control Number: 2019905535

Cover Photo © 2019 www.gettyimages.com.. All rights reserved - used with permission.

Outskirts Press and the "OP" logo are trademarks belonging to Outskirts Press, Inc.

PRINTED IN THE UNITED STATES OF AMERICA

With love and appreciation to my dear husband, Gene,
and
with gratitude to the Oklahoma City Dead Writers.

WHAT THE CAT DRAGGED IN is a collection of short stories, poems and personal essays written during the past several years. Many have been published, and most have won prizes in literary contests. It is with pleasure that I share them with my readers in this volume.

Table of Contents

SHORT STORIES

AUNT JIM'S CORNBREAD DRESSING	2
ROUND TRIP	5
JUST DESERTS	25
DESOLATION	36
THE OLD RUGGED CROSS	43
ON TOP OF OLD SMOKEY	57
A DROWNING: SUMMER, 1944	77
QUEENIE ADAMS: Ladies in Waiting	83
RETRIBUTION	106
LOVE, SQUALOR, AND THE MEXICAN MEN	113
A PERFECT WEDDING FOR EMILY	127
THE ELEPHANT MOUND	144
A STORY OF AN HOUR	151
THE PIG MAN	157
THE CHRISTMAS PARTY SEND-OFF	170

POETRY

SUMMERTIME GIRLS, 1960	196
ABSTRACT ART	198
THE CRITIC	199
THE SUMMER OF OUR DISCONTENT	200
X	202
OCTOBER HAYSTACKS	204
THE FUNERAL OF A FIRST HUSBAND	205
SARAH PEARL HAMMOND	207

THE ELEPHANT AND THE CAT	209
THE WHEELER CEMETERY	211
GRIEF	213
QUANDRY	214
AS WE BECOME OUR MOTHERS	216
THE BLACK MADONNAS	218

ESSAYS

CHRISTMAS EVE IN SENEGAL	222
ALL LAID OUT	225
LONG LIVE THE SWEET POTATO QUEENS	228
THE GRAND PASSION OF DESPERATE HOUSECATS	232
ARE MEN NECESSARY?	237
NOT EVEN IN A HANDBASKET	241
A SKUNK BY ANY OTHER NAME WOULD SMELL AS SWEET	245
I FEEL BAD ABOUT MY WHATCHAMACALLIT	250
LEAPIN' LIZARDS!	253
THE HUMILIATION CLINIC	257
I DREAMED I KISSED SANTA CLAUS	260
AIN'T NO CURE FOR THE SUMMERTIME BLUES	264
THE DEVIL CARRIES PRADA	268
PECKED TO DEATH	272
MEN ARE LIKE GRAPES	275
RAISE YOUR GLASS TO MOTHERHOOD	279
THE CAPTAIN'S TABLE	282

SHORT STORIES

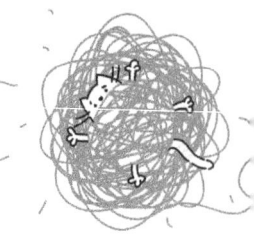

AUNT JIM'S CORNBREAD DRESSING

My Aunt Jim Crump made the best cornbread dressing you ever put in your mouth. Umm-umm! So good it made you want to slap your grandma.

She was my great aunt and she kept a secret recipe. Because of some unknown ingredient, her dressing far surpassed anybody else's. This caused my mother and our other women relatives to stew.

Every Thanksgiving Mother sneaked into Aunt Jim's kitchen to find out what made her dressing so good. But Aunt Jim was too quick for her, always having made it before we arrived.

Every year, at the dinner table Mother would say, "Oh, Aunt Jim, your dressing is the best in the whole wide world. What's your secret?"

Aunt Jim answered, "Oh, pshaw, honey. My dressing is just like everyone else's. No secret at all." Then she'd laugh with pleasure.

So, Mother went home, made turkey and dressing a month later at Christmas, and her dressing turned out dry and tasteless. It was the same story for all the women in the family. And they got seriously annoyed with old Aunt Jim.

"She should share what she knows!" they said. "What if we made dressing like that dreadful stuff they make up North? Everybody knows Yankees can't make dressing worth a flip! If we were cooking up that nasty wet gray stuff, wouldn't she want to help us out? Of course, she would! So why won't she help us now? She's so stubborn she'll carry that cornbread dressing secret to the grave!" Every time they talked about it, they worked themselves into a tizzy.

When I was fourteen, my mother, her sister Samantha and our cousin Mary devised a plan to learn the truth about Aunt Jim's cornbread dressing. They talked me into offering to help our aunt prepare the meal. My job was to go to her house early and work in her kitchen before anybody else arrived. I was to snoop around, go through the trash if necessary, and carefully watch as our aunt prepared the dressing.

These women were naïve enough to think that Aunt Jim wouldn't know what I was up to. I didn't want to do it.

But Mother was used to having her own way. She had worked herself into a frenzy, and she was desperate.

"If you'll get the recipe for your Aunt Jim's dressing, I'll buy you a mouton coat," she said.

More than anything in the world, I wanted a mouton coat. So, I agreed to spy and steal the recipe. Early that

Thanksgiving morning, I went to Aunt Jim's house.

Here's her recipe: Crumble a big pan of cornbread, not too fine, and stir in a package of herb-seasoned dried breadcrumbs. Add about a cup each of chopped celery and onion sautéed in butter together. Stir in three eggs and four cans of chicken broth. Finally, add salt, pepper, and sage to taste. Bake 30-40 minutes at 350 degrees.

"The secret ingredient is the canned chicken broth," Aunt Jim told me. "But you won't tell your mother, will you?"

"No, ma'am, I guess not." I was horrified at her question.

"What did she promise you to come here and find out?"

"A mouton coat."

"I can't afford a coat. I'll rely on your sense of honor," she said.

"Yes, ma'am," I said, mentally kissing the coat goodbye.

So ultimately, I wound up lying to my mother.

"There's no secret ingredient," I told her when she quizzed me while we drove home from the feast. "Aunt Jim makes her dressing just like you do."

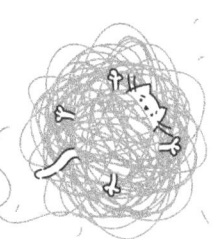

ROUND TRIP

Maria panics every time I tell her the Germans are coming. I don't know why she gets upset; she certainly stays calm when I'm preparing for other guests. But the idea of Germans coming to our place and staying in our town — even if it's just overnight — frightens her.

I don't want to scare Maria, because she's the only good thing to come my way since I moved to Missouri five years ago. Actually, moved against my will — it was my husband's idea.

"Wouldn't it be a great thing to do with the house we inherited," Sam argued, "to turn it into a bed and breakfast inn, in the heart of the Ozark Mountains?" When he got on a tangent, which he did with this B & B plan, trying to change his mind was useless.

"You can cook, and I'll do cleaning and handy-man jobs," he said. "We'll turn that Victorian monstrosity into a money-maker."

Finally, I agreed — never fully believing in the project — and we moved from our retirement home in Florida into this place, surrounded by wildlife, water, and pines. We worked like hell, renovating what had been his grandmother's Missouri home, just off old Route 66. Now the house is beautiful, with four stories, including the basement and the attic.

For our personal privacy, Sam and I built an apartment over the carriage-house, away from the main building. From our suite we looked out over the valley. Pretending to live in a tree house, we were surrounded by black walnuts, oaks, and maples. Laughing, we agreed that if we weren't so damned exhausted and old, our getaway would be romantic. We called it "The Bower."

After slaving over the inherited house for a year, we started taking in tourists. Turned out to be a lot more effort and worry than Sam expected. In a couple of years, we were about to admit to each other — I, sooner than he — that this venture wasn't good for two aging retired public schoolteachers. Then one night, after a sudden massive heart attack, Sam died.

I want to sell the place. Have listed it with a realtor and advertised everywhere. But in the meantime, I must live, and in the throes of almost overwhelming fear, I finally decided to get help and try to make a go of The Ozarks Dogwood Inn. So, I approached a group of Hispanic people in our small town and explained my need to hire a handyman/janitor/helper/cook. That's how I found the talented Maria, who fills all these roles beautifully.

When I inform her that German guests are coming, she says, "I stay in kitchen. You serve."

And that's that.

The German tourists are crazy about visiting America.

They usually fly in small groups from Frankfurt to the East Coast and spend some time in New York City or D.C. Then they fly to Chicago, buy motorcycles, and start driving down historic Route 66, usually all the way to California. Not just men, but women, also. They arrive at our inn late in the day, covered with dirt, black leather clothes and all, ready for beer, which they sometimes bring themselves – dark German beer, purchased in Chicago, strapped to the backs of their motorcycles.

They're loud but polite, and they're always curious about points of interest along the way. So, I've prepared a mini-history lesson about Route 66, along with slides, which I present in the parlor every evening after supper, while Maria washes dishes in the kitchen.

I'm impressed by the Germans. Never would you see one of these guests wear a t-shirt with a slogan on the back that says, "If you can read this, the bitch fell off."

Oh, no, but some of our American guests wear that slogan with hoggish pride. So, I prefer the Germans, for that and other reasons, one being that they're interested in my slide show. Also, they seem to appreciate our history, our land, and the food we serve. They're clean, they leave their rooms in order, and they tell their friends about us when they return home. So, every year we get a fresh supply of German guests. They come late in the day, spend the night, and leave the next morning on their cycles.

When Gustav Schindler and his wife, Gretchen, arrive, it is in the spring, and the mountains are covered with pink and white dogwoods. The Schindlers are accompanied by two other couples. Gustav is large and boisterous, but Gretchen is pale and thin, as quiet as a small bird hiding in the forest. I wonder if something's wrong with her, not just because of her gauntness, but also because she gazes off during a conversation, inattentive to people around. During dinner, she sits at the table with the others, not eating much, not joining in the jokes and laughter, and I wonder if she's sad or angry or perhaps even homesick. I want to ask if there's maybe something I can fix. Doesn't she like the food? Is her room uncomfortable? Does she understand our language? That's a stupid question, because the Germans speak their own language exclusively when conversing with each other, even with other diners around. Still, all is obviously not right with Gretchen, and as the hostess of Dogwood Inn, I feel compelled to learn what it is.

While our guests enjoy their meal in the dining room, I decide to ask Maria to help me serve. She refuses, so I confront her with the issue of why she will have nothing to do with Germans.

"Why do you fear them? Is it because they speak their own language most of the time?" I ask, *sotto voce*.

"I do not fear Germans," she mutters. "But they are bad people."

"How can you tell?"

"I know what they did, what they do. You serve, you talk to them. I stay in the kitchen to cook and clean. Do not ask me to serve Germans."

"You actually hate those people. I don't understand why."

"Too rich. Too loud. Think they're better than us."

"Better than who? You and me?"

"Better than Mexicans." She pauses. "Better than everybody."

I ask Maria to come out of the kitchen to observe Gretchen, to help me decide what's the matter with this silent forlorn woman, so detached from her partying husband and traveling companions. But Maria refuses to do that, also.

Finally, later in the evening, after my slide show, I catch Gustav in the hall.

"Is your wife ill?" I ask. "Is she not enjoying her trip?"

"She is fine," he answers. "She's happy with our journey. She's the one who wanted to come to the U.S. of A."

The next day, when they leave, he gives me a warm hug.

"Friends for life," he says. He and Gretchen climb onto his Harley; she, riding behind him. Starting the motor, he stomps on the gas pedal. Clinging to her husband, Gretchen never looks my way.

Maria's husband beats her. I know that, because when I first saw the bruises, I questioned her. In the heat of a summer day, she'd taken off a long-sleeved shirt, and she stood at the washing machine, loading it with sheets. She wore a sleeveless t-shirt, and I could see bruises on her arms and shoulders. Her long, dark hair hung down, and her back was to me. I walked over to her. Treating her like a child, I lifted her hair and saw that her neck was dark, swollen.

"What happened?"

She shrugged and moved away.

"Did Carlos do this?"

No answer.

"Maria, if you were my daughter, I'd want somebody to help you. Tell me what to do."

"There's nothing anyone can do," she answered.

"Does Carlos hit the children?"

"Not as much as he hits me."

"You should go to the sheriff. I'll go with you."

"Ha!" She snorted. She finished loading the machine, turned it on and left the room.

How little I know about the people in my life. I have only miniscule amounts of information concerning the people who stay in my house, even those who come often to enjoy the beauty of our changing seasons. I have their names, addresses, telephone numbers and email addresses. Sometimes the names of their next of kin. I usually learn what their professions are and occasionally tidbits about their families. Often, I hear more than I want to know about my guests' health, religion, or political persuasion. But I never know anyone's favorite color. Or piece of music. Or what they dreamed of becoming, as children. Or what they truly love. As for their marriages, I see only superficial snippets.

It's a shame to know so little about these people, but it's worse to know so little about the woman who works for me, day after day. This beautiful, bright young woman has saved my life – my sanity at least – by helping me out during my rough times without Sam.

Convinced that I must do something to help Maria, one day I offer to let her and the children stay with me.

"You don't know what you're saying," she answers.

"You can live here as long as you like. Who knows? Maybe Carlos will learn to control his temper and after a while you can go back to him."

"You don't understand. I need him."

Sadly, this is true. She needs him with his paltry paycheck from the chicken plant to provide for their three children. She needs his insurance and retirement, because I can't afford to supply these things. I'm partly responsible for her troubles, because of the pittance I pay her. I'm the one who really won't help Maria.

I ponder about these problems, worry because I'm not doing enough, and feel guilty that I'm not able to do more. In the meantime, we entertain bed and breakfast guests every night and clean up after them each morning. The summer slowly moves along.

In the fall, when outrageous color bursts from the mountains in red, orange and golden splotches, Gustav and Gretchen Schindler return. This time, they travel alone, and not by motorcycle, but in a comfortable, leather-lined sedan. The jolly Gustav greets me with a hug.

"My friend for life," he says. But Gretchen is even more pale, more shrunken, more silent, than before. She wears a large blonde wig, like a ladies' mannequin. The truth immediately settles on me. Gretchen has been treated for cancer.

At dinnertime, guests fill our dining room. I've seated the Schindlers beside one of the windows, hoping that in the fading light they can gaze out at the copper maples and bright red sumac.

Gretchen eats very little. When she finishes, she tries to rise, but her legs buckle, and she collapses. Standing near their table, I reach to catch her, but she's dead weight. Clinging to each other, we both go down. The other diners cry out as Gustav pulls me up, and suddenly Maria is there, with her arms around Gretchen. She and Gustav lift the sick woman. Gretchen's feet, like useless twigs, drag the floor as Maria and Gustav, so different in size and substance, try to carry her. Then another male guest moves in to help. Gustav, the other gentleman, and Maria take Gretchen upstairs.

Later, after getting Gretchen settled, Gustav slides into the kitchen, where Maria and I work. She stands at the sink, peeling vegetables for tomorrow's pot roast, refusing to turn around. In the quietest voice possible, Gustav confirms my diagnosis of cancer. He and Gretchen have spent the summer in Houston at M.D. Anderson Hospital, where she underwent treatments. What started as a single malfunctioning sick cell in a breast has spread throughout her body. Regardless of what science and excellent doctors can do, Gretchen will die soon.

"Gretchen wanted to get back on Route 66," he says. "We drive to Chicago and then fly home. A round trip."

"A round trip," I repeat. "Oh, Gustav, I'm so sorry for you both."

Knowing what Gustav will face without his wife, I want to weep. I look over at Maria, who continues to wash her vegetables.

The next morning, Gustav comes to me. "My wife is weak for travel," he says. "We wish to spend this day resting. Can you accommodate us?"

With a little finagling, I'm able to let them keep their room.

I'm putting up groceries in the pantry. Not knowing of her aversion to Germans, Gustav comes into the kitchen and asks Maria to stay with Gretchen while he goes to buy gas. She answers yes and I watch her follow him up the stairs to the Schindlers' bedroom. Gustav is gone for less than half an hour. When he returns, he immediately goes back upstairs. The sound of voices with Spanish and German accents wafts down to me, but I can't decipher their conversation.

Just before dinner, I suggest that the Schindlers have their meal in their room, and he agrees to do so. I prepare the trays, and Maria carries them upstairs. Later, Gustav comes downstairs to watch my slide show "one last time." Paying no mind to the rest of us, Maria continues working in the kitchen.

I wake up in the middle of the night. The crisp, still autumn air has turned cool, and I get up to close my window. That's when I hear the sound. At first, I think it's an animal, but then I realize it's someone weeping. That or someone making love.

Looking from my upstairs carriage-house room

toward the main lodging, I see no lights in any of the windows. Where are the strange sounds coming from? I decide it must be Gretchen, truly in pain, truly miserable.

The next morning Maria is late coming to work, so I prepare breakfast for our guests by myself. I put aside my irritation with her, concentrating on eggs benedict and hollandaise sauce, which is a trial for me. Yet, I want Gretchen and Gustav to have the best I can give them before their long drive.

I serve them, along with the other guests, and we talk about the beauty of the Ozark mountains during autumn as compared with the spring. All superficial, all meaningless chatter.

When the Schindlers walk out the front door, down the steps from the veranda toward their automobile, I'm overcome by sadness, and follow close behind. Putting my arm around Gretchen, I make her turn to me, and I embrace her.

Then Gustav grabs me, gives his bear-hug and laughs, "Friends forever." He helps Gretchen into the backseat of the car, gently settling her on a bed he's made, and then they're gone.

When I go back inside, Maria has returned and is cleaning up from breakfast. I look at her face, swollen and bruised.

"You and your kids should come live here," I say.

"If we did, Carlos would kill me," she answers.

"Not if you're with me. Surely you'd be safe."

"You don't know Carlos."

Maria and I have fewer guests during the fall. For Thanksgiving week, business picks up, and we work ourselves into a frenzy, preparing food for people who want a holiday retreat. Same during Christmas week. One obstreperous family spends five days with us, eating everything we can prepare, playing games, the losers screaming at the winners, spilling drinks, making messes. For New Year's it's the same, this time with couples. What's their fascination with this place? Obviously, Maria and I spoil them; we make things too comfortable. Although I need the money, I wish all these people would go home.

By the second week in January, folks have cleared out, and we'll have some time to refurbish, clean things up, breathe, and relax, before the onslaught in the spring. Still no buyers for my B & B. The only thing in the world I truly want is to get rid of this backbreaking, heartbreaking place.

One day Maria informs me that we have rats in the attic and the basement.

"You need to call Murphy's Feed and Seed," she says, "and see what they recommend."

"Rats? Are you sure? I haven't seen them," I say.

"That or large mice," she answers. "Do you want to see droppings?"

I call Murphy, place my order, and Maria goes to town to buy the poison. Bringing back three boxes, she puts it out.

"Stay out of attic and basement," she tells me. "This poison will take care of the problem."

For weeks we have no bed and breakfast guests scheduled. I'm invited to visit my children in Florida, so I close the place for the month of February, and Maria signs on at the chicken plant to work nights. She'll continue to check on things for me, but at minimum salary.

"Keep the houseplants fed and the rats dead," I laugh, as I pack my suitcases.

She assures me she'll do just that.

When I return to Missouri during the first week in March, the weather is still fiercely cold.

"No chance that we'll have B & B guests until the mountains warm up significantly," I say to Maria over the telephone. I tell her to keep her job at the chicken plant for a while.

I begin the project of cleaning the old Victorian house, starting with the basement. Sweeping and carrying trash away, I find many things that Sam and I saved through the years, but I don't want now. I find no evidence of rats. Nor do I find any poison.

I'm curious. Why was Maria so certain about the rats? I begin looking everywhere – under mattresses, inside closets, around the draperies, in the pantry, anywhere there is interesting fabric to gnaw on, good places to build nests, or even a morsel of food to eat. I find no sign of rats. I think about calling Maria and telling her, but then I forget and don't do it.

By the first of April, we're having guests again. One evening Maria brings her calendar, and we sit down to match our schedules. Understandably, she doesn't want to give up her night job at the chicken plant until I can afford to hire her fulltime again.

Something about her has changed. She's less nervous than she was a few months ago.

"How are things at home?" I ask.

"Oh, fine," she says.

"The kids?"

"Kids are great."

"And Carlos?"

"Carlos is sick."

"Oh?"

"Stomach trouble," she answers, looking at me straight on.

"What's the matter with him?"

"Doctor doesn't know. But I think cancer."

How do you voice your suspicions to a person you love and trust? How do you say, "Maria, I hope you aren't killing your husband"? How do you say, "I don't blame you for trying, but this isn't the way to get out of your terrible situation"? How do you simply ask, "What the hell did you do with all that rat poison?"

Maybe you say nothing. Just decide to ride it out and see what happens. Maybe knowing nothing is better than knowing everything.

I say nothing, and I wait.

Three weeks later, Carlos is dead. The Catholic funeral ceremony is long and laborious, and I'm one of the few non-Hispanics who attend. I watch the beautiful Maria, my daughter's age, dressed in a black dress I've given her and altered myself. She wears a black lace shawl over her head, the mantilla Sam bought for me when we visited Mexico, a long time ago. Her children, the same ages as my grandchildren, dressed in church clothes that I've rounded up for them, weep for their father, Carlos, the man I never really knew but absolutely detested.

What would Sam say about all of this? How would he react to my suspicions? Enthusiastic, optimistic, unrealistic Sam would tell me I'm insane.

This spring, we're busier than ever. All the rooms in my B & B are booked every night, and Maria and I hardly have time to think, much less have a conversation. I talk to myself frequently, like a very old woman, trying to persuade myself that nothing sinister has occurred. But while planting impatiens around the patio, in amongst the azalea bushes Sam planted years ago, I uncover three empty rat poison boxes.

After the shock of finding them, I rebury them – under the impatiens. Does this make me an accessory to a crime? Shaking, I imagine a weird courtroom scene with a judge telling me, "You must answer the question. Were you aware of the empty rat poison boxes buried among your azaleas?"

For days, when my thoughts jump to Carlos and the poison, I make my mind behave, make it come back to the present business of the day, and I say nothing. And Maria doesn't mention the location of my plantings. But she praises my gardening and compliments my impatiens mightily.

I'm standing in my bedroom at dusk, having gone upstairs to change clothes before serving dinner, and I look through the lacy leaves of the trees outside my window. I see Maria below, standing next to a man who is much taller than she. He puts his right arm on her shoulder, slides his hand down her arm, takes her hand and pulls her toward him. Bending over, he kisses her, long, lovingly. Then she pulls away. I think I can hear her laugh. From above, I don't recognize this man, but he doesn't look Hispanic.

Less than an hour later, an expected band of Germans arrives. All men. Gustav Schindler is among them. Loud and funny, they eat voraciously, tell jokes in German, and sing the lyrics to the old TV Route 66 song in English. "Get your kicks down Route sixty-six!"

At the end of the evening, they applaud my slide show. They've made me feel chipper and witty, and I thank them for it. Gustav grabs me, gives me a hug and then rushes into the kitchen to compliment Maria on their meal. I follow him.

It's obvious that Gustav and Maria know each other well. Gone is her reticence to associate with Germans. He reaches for her hand and pulls her toward him, and I realize he's the man she was kissing out under the trees.

"Good God in heaven, when did this begin?" I ask.

They look at me, step apart quickly, and then act as if nothing has happened between them. They pretend not to have heard my question.

The next morning, after all the guests, including the

Germans, have left, I walk into the laundry room and confront Maria.

"Please tell me what's going on," I say.

"What do you mean?"

"With Gustav. What is it with you and Gustav?"

"You know I can't be without a man," she shrugs.

"Ridiculous! Look at *me*. I live without a man."

"Yes, and look at you," she answers.

I ignore the insult and ask, "When did you decide to like Germans?"

"When I get to know them better."

"And when did that happen?"

"When did what happen?" She smiles, mysteriously.

Now my thoughts and feelings toward Maria are ambiguous. I don't know what to expect from her. I remember a newspaper article I once read about a man in Arkansas who shot and killed his wife with a crossbow. His horrified neighbors told reporters that up until the moment of the murder, he was a "very nice man." I shudder and go to the parlor to lie down. I hear Maria moving from room to room, following our daily routine, humming tunelessly. As I listen, I feel old and unsure.

A month later, Gustav is back. Unexpected, he simply shows up at the front door. Standing on the veranda, wearing his black clothes, sunglasses, and a red bandana, he smiles. Alone this time, he travels on an enormous new Harley.

"Do you have a room for me?" he wants to know, wearing glasses that reflect my absurd, distorted image.

"I don't know what to say, Gustav. I'm all booked up. I had no idea you were making another round trip."

"I would like a drink of water. I will wait in the parlor. Perhaps you will discover a way to accommodate me." He smiles.

I go upstairs, talk to Maria, who is making beds. She and I decide to bring down an old rollaway from the attic and set it up for another guest, a little boy. Gustav helps us move it downstairs to the child's parents' room. We assign Gustav what had been the child's room, and lock the adjoining door, thus giving Gustav a small room with privacy. While Maria makes his bed, he thanks me.

"What is it you Americans say? 'Where there's a will, there's a way.' Is that it?" he asks, smiling.

Gustav is as undaunted and as optimistic as Sam was.

He stays for several days. Sometimes he goes out on his cycle, exploring the territory, and comes in with additional facts and notions to add to my slide show commentary. But many days, he says around and helps Maria and me with chores. He never mentions Gretchen, so one morning I ask him about her.

"So much suffering," he says, his eyes filling with tears. "The end – terrible."

In helping us, Gustav can often improve upon the way we do things, a habit that Maria welcomes, and I resent. Despite all his help, I find myself wondering when he'll leave.

One morning, after all the guests except Gustav have gone, Maria says, "We want to talk to you."

We three walk into the parlor and sit, and Gustav says, "I want to buy your place. I want to have a farm and a vineyard. The very first time I see it, I know this is what I want."

"How does Maria figure into this?" I ask.

"Oh, I want Maria, too. 'The whole shooting match,' as you Americans would say."

Maria tells me, "You could stay here. You could live in Gustav's little room and still serve as hostess. We won't pay much, but you can stay as long as you want."

"Who will live in the Bower?"

"We will," she says.

"I buy this place outright at good price," Gustav says, naming the amount he'll pay.

His is the only offer I've received. I tell him I'll think it over.

Later in the day, I sit in my bedroom, looking out over the valley, my windows sheltered by the late summer leaves of the black walnut tree. A large brown squirrel appears. Standing on the limb, he twitches his tail as he looks through the window and watches me closely.

"What am I to do?" I ask him. Fortunately, he doesn't answer, which proves that perhaps I'm not a lunatic after all.

I awake at about 4:00 a.m., my head crowded with questions. When did Maria and Gustav get to know one another? What were the sounds I heard the night before he and Gretchen left my B & B? Did Maria approach Gustav that night and ask for his help? Did she stay with him until late? Making love? Weeping? Did she return home to an enraged Carlos, who beat her so badly she resolved to rid herself of him forever? Then did she actually poison Carlos? And with Gustav's knowledge?

Apparently, the doctor didn't think Carlos died of poison. But maybe the doctor knows the truth as well as I, that Carlos was violent and cruel. No, if the doctor had suspected Maria of murder, surely, he would have called the sheriff.

I disapprove of Carlos' murder almost as much as I disapproved of Carlos.

I sell the B & B to Gustav. He buys adjoining property, additional acreage for his vineyards. Soon after I've signed the papers and collected the money, my sons come from Florida, help me pack, and take off in a U-Haul. I insist on staying for another day or two; then I'll drive to Florida and live there. For the rest of my days.

One morning before I go, as I'm putting my things in order, I look up to see Maria, standing in the doorway of my bedroom. We are surrounded by golden light, bird sounds, tree branches and leaves.

"We really wanted you to stay," she tells me.

"I appreciate the offer, but at some point, you'd be sick of me," I answer.

"Perhaps, but not for a long time."

"And then what would you do? Poison me?"

She walks over to me. Patting my cheek, she looks into my eyes and smiles.

"Dear friend, you are not well," she says.

After packing my car, I tell them goodbye.

"Friends forever," says Gustav, hugging me, "if you ever miss us, come back to this old place."

Maria says nothing. Her embrace is shallow.

Sitting in the front seat of my car, I look at them: Gustav – tall, strong, dressed in black, and Maria – small, wearing pink Capri pants and a pink striped shirt. Standing on the porch against the blue house framed by white gingerbread trim, Gustav has his arm around Maria, and they both smile and wave. Her hair in braids, she looks like a schoolgirl, waving at a tired old woman.

For the last time, I drive into town, where I've traveled so often during the last five years. Today I park my car in front of the sheriff's office. I'm sorry about Carlos' murder and wish I didn't know what I know. Surely, I should share that information. Surely, I'm an accessory to a crime. But then I recall how satisfied Maria looked as I drove away.

I remember she once told me, *"You know I can't be without a man."*

In the distance, I hear a motorcycle. It's coming closer.

Putting the car in reverse, I back out of my parking space. Then I drive on.

JUST DESERTS

On board the cruise ship *The Felicity*, the elderly man rose to his feet at the round dining table. Surrounded by seven fellow passengers, he turned to the waitress, a slender, tall blond Finnish girl with a braid halfway down her back.

"Gorgeous!" the old man yelled, reaching upward with his right hand holding a glass of red wine. Then he lurched toward the girl. She shrieked and jumped away, and the man fell, crashing to the floor with a linen napkin in one hand and a wineglass in the other.

Putting her hands to her face, the waitress began to cry, as the other diners tried to squirm around the table to help the fallen passenger. But he had already passed out, unaware of the scene he had caused.

The old man was dead-dog drunk.

The trip to Russia had been Annie's idea. "It's on my Bucket List," she had told her husband, Robert. "I've always wanted to see the Kremlin. And I'm dying to visit the Hermitage."

"I didn't know you had a Bucket List," Robert said.

"Since that movie with Jack Nicholson and Morgan

Freeman came out, everybody has a Bucket List," she told him. "Everybody our age, at least."

Seventy-year-old Robert Fulton looked glum. "I have no desire to visit Russia," he said. "I can give you a hundred reasons why it's not a good idea, starting out with the fact that we can't afford it."

"According to you, we can't afford anything," she said. "Have you ever noticed how truly stingy you are?" *Watch out, Annie*, she told herself. *This is no way to get to the Land of the Czars.*

After several months, Robert changed his mind and announced that he wanted to go to Russia. He made this decision after spending an evening with old fraternity brothers, playing poker, smoking cigars and drinking vodka. His friends, retired, round and jocular, expressed surprise that he and Annie had never taken a Russian cruise.

"You really must go there before you die," they told him. "Take a river cruise."

So, the day after the poker party, Robert suggested to Annie that they take a Russian river cruise. As far as he was concerned, it was entirely his idea. Annie quickly made reservations, before he could change his mind.

After their arrival in St. Petersburg, late in the afternoon, Robert and Annie were taken straight to their cruise ship, *The Felicity*, which would remain docked for three days, while the passengers toured the city.

Having dragged their luggage into their cabin, Robert and Annie inspected the room and unpacked their things.

"This place is pretty damned cramped," he complained.

"You get larger quarters if you're willing to pay more money," Annie said. "Of course, it's too late now. Let's try to be happy with it." Finishing the unpacking, she said, "Let's go to Happy Hour."

In the bar, Ed and Sandra Grosman sat together under a large window that looked out toward the city. Except for the bartender, the room was empty, so the Grosmans invited the Fultons to join them. The Grosmans were the first people on the tour that Annie and Robert met. The Perfect Match, Annie thought. Same age (seventy!), both men retired (businessmen!), same interests (fishing!), same political affiliation (Republican!), same church preference (Episcopalian!), same number of grandchildren (eight!). Also, the Grosmans were interesting and funny.

"Hey, have you heard this one…," Ed Grosman had the habit of saying, before dipping into his repertoire of stories.

After a couple of drinks, the two couples ambled from the bar to the dining room together. Grey-headed and round, they looked like two sets of elderly Humpty-Dumpty dolls, waddling down the ship's corridors.

But at the end of the evening, on the way back to their cabin, Robert told Annie, "Don't get in the clutches of those people again. I don't like them. They both talk too much."

On the first day of their trip in St. Petersburg, they explored the Hermitage.

"What's he saying?" Robert asked Annie repeatedly,

referring to their guide. She noticed Robert had neglected to wear his hearing aids.

"My hearing aids bother me," he told her, after she questioned him. "You'll just have to tell me what the guides say about all this stuff. Besides, I really don't need the damned things. I did fine without them on the plane."

"Are you telling me you didn't bring your hearing aids on this trip?" she whispered, afraid of interrupting the guide's lecture.

"I told you they drive me crazy!" he growled.

When their guide offered to let the group have extra time to view additional art exhibits, Robert sighed, "I'm tired. I've seen enough."

He returned to his seat on the bus while Annie toured the museum with the others.

The next day the group rode another large bus out of St. Petersburg, to the small-town Pushkin, to visit the Palace of Catherine the Great.

Walking through the Great Hall, Robert was perplexed. "What the hell are these people saying?" he grumbled. "They have terrible accents, and they mumble!"

"Oh, Robert," Annie said, as she snapped pictures of the first huge mirrored room, heavily decorated with golden rococo statuary. "Look at the elegance of this place. Look at all this gold!"

"Gaudy and ostentatious," he said. "No wonder there was a revolution."

After the tour of the palace, the group was given free time before meeting in the garden. When Anne stopped at the museum store to buy amber jewelry for their granddaughters, Robert refused to go inside.

"For God's sake, hurry!" he ordered. "You shouldn't buy this junk anyway."

Back on the boat, before every meal—breakfast, lunch and dinner—the Fultons avoided the Grosmans. They sat with a variety of other people, some of whom Annie regarded as potential friends. But after three days Robert had compiled a list of everyone he wished to avoid. The list included not only the Grosmans but also the Russells and Beverly White (who traveled with the Russells)—*a ménage trois*, Robert was sure. In addition, he couldn't stand the Simpsons (obsessive about health and disease), the Tates (unfriendly snobs), the O'Reillys (obviously Catholic) or the Jacksons (Democrats).

"There are only a hundred and fifty people on this boat, Robert," Annie commented. "Pretty soon we'll run out of people to sit with."

But before every meal, walking through the dining room he followed Annie closely, grumbling instructions into her ear about where they should sit. Unfortunately, he never found seating partners that lived up to his expectations.

On the last evening in St. Petersburg, the tour group traveled back to the Hermitage, this time to the Catherine Theater to see *Swan Lake*.

"Oh, brother," Robert moaned. "Just what I need—a sissy ballet, with grown men wearing tutus. What kind of a man would wear a leotard? Only a damned fairy."

That night the cruise ship left St. Petersburg and headed down a series of rivers toward Moscow.

"Goodbye and good riddance to old St. Petersburg," Robert said, looking out the dining room window. "What ungodly traffic. And the dilapidated apartment houses! Jeez!"

Moving along, the ship made daily stops at various towns along the way. For their tours off the ship, Annie carried everything they needed in a huge red hobo tote. Money, guidebooks, cameras, Robert's cell phone (although it didn't work in Russia), maps, a spiral notebook, pens, sunglasses, a scarf for her, a cap for him, lipstick, chap stick, tissues, a Russian dictionary, a box of power snack bars, and an apple Robert swiped from the fruit display at the breakfast buffet every morning.

Most important, she carried two passes—one for her and one for Robert—which the ship's captain gave to the passengers every day as they left the boat. At the end of the day, these passes were collected by the captain's crew as each passenger came back on board. This allowed the crew to match the passes with the passengers, thus affirming that everyone was accounted for, before lifting anchor and sailing away.

On the first night of the actual cruise, the young, handsome captain stressed the importance of each passenger being responsible for his own pass.

In halting English, the captain told them, "Please to take your ticket. You and you only. We never want a mistake to make. We never want to leave you behind."

"What a rube. Why doesn't he learn to speak English?" Robert complained.

Cruising on the Svir River toward the River Volga, Annie developed an acute ache in her left jaw. She'd had it before, a result of grinding her teeth in her sleep. What's more, now she awoke every morning with a headache and a stiff neck, a result, she was sure, of carrying her bagful of necessities.

"Robert, how about helping me with my handbag?" she asked on day. "Think you might carry it for a while?"

"Are you crazy? Me carry a purse?"

"It's giving me a terrible shoulder ache."

"Oh, all right! Jiminy Christmas!" He slung it over his shoulder like a sack of flour.

"Never mind," Annie said, taking the bag from him. "I don't want you to crash into anything."

Then one night Robert's personality changed. The Fultons were seated with three new couples—the Andrews, the Smiths, and the Spieldings—none of whom they'd met before. Wine flowed quite freely. Robert became cheerful and charming. Standing up and raising a full glass (probably his sixth), he said, "I want to toast the ship, the captain, and the crew. This is the best goddamn cruise in the world! Gorgeous!"

That's when Robert reached for the delectable blonde waitress from Finland. His right arm shot out and grabbed her fanny. She jumped. And then he fell with a crash to the floor. In alarm, everyone at the table rose to their feet. Surely Robert had suffered a heart attack. In those first few horrible moments, Annie was afraid he might die. And then she was afraid he might not.

For immediately, after crouching on her knees beside him, Annie realized that Robert was only drunk. With help from one of the waiters, she gathered her husband up off the floor and then, together, she and the young man walked Robert to their room. They put him to bed.

Annie felt as if she were cruising down the river of Hell, all cooped up with Robert, amid strangers who would have nothing to do with them, since Robert was managing to insult everyone, right and left, as quickly as he could. When did this misery begin? On the plane from the U.S.? With Robert's loud, self-righteous comments on board about the food, the space (or lack thereof), the other passengers, the choice of movies?

No, it began long before this trip. Years ago, maybe from the moment they met, maybe even before they met. He was a horse's ass. How could she not have known? How could she be such an utter fool? She'd spent fifty years with a man not worth shooting. And only now, trapped on a small cruise ship with him, was she forced to deal with his totally impossible ways.

Annie vowed to revise her Bucket List. When she got home, back in the States, she would add, "Outlive Robert."

"Well, you certainly took a long time in the bathroom," Robert said when he awoke from his stupor. "Taking a shower shouldn't be that complicated. Why are you so slow?"

"I don't know, Robert. It's just the way I am."

He rolled over and went back to sleep.

Early the next morning, the ship docked at Svirstroy, a tiny, isolated village with a population of about a hundred people, with a few dogs and cats to keep them company.

"Looks like a penal colony," Robert announced, as he looked out the window at the pastoral scene. He threw three aspirin down his throat and took a swig of bottled water.

Outside, the tourists were divided into small groups and then met onshore by local guides, who led them to townspeople's homes for tea. Robert refused to go with Annie.

"I don't give a damn about seeing how these people live," he told her.

"What will you do?" she asked.

"I'll wander around the place. What time do we go back to the ship?"

Annie hesitated. Reaching into her big red bag, she pulled out their schedule and checked. It clearly said, "Three-thirty."

"Four-thirty," she told Robert, looking into his eyes.

Over the loud speaker the captain had already reminded everyone that they should be back on board by 3:30 pm at the latest. Apparently, Robert hadn't heard the announcement. Her heart raced as she looked again at her husband.

"I'll wait for you on the dock at four-thirty," she said.

"I saw some fishermen back a ways on the shore.

Think I'll go check out what they're catching," he said.

"Excellent idea, Robert." Annie thought she might have heart failure as she watched him walk away.

He turned around and yelled, "Don't be late. Remember, we both must show our passes to get back on board. And you have mine!"

"Yes, I know, Robert," she called, and turned to catch up with her assigned group.

Annie enjoyed her visit to a tiny wooden cottage, badly in need of paint, but charming, nonetheless. It was set in the center of a wildly fragrant and fertile vegetable garden. Inside the cottage she met a smiling hostess, who welcomed the American visitors and served tea. Wearing a ruffled magenta print dress and pearls, the elderly white-haired lady spoke Russian to her guests as the guide translated.

"Welcome to my home, you beautiful American people," she said. Then she sang a spirited folk song for them and they applauded.

Annie was glad that Robert wasn't there to ruin the occasion.

The tourists met on the dock at 3:15. They moved *en masse* up the gangplank. As she approached the crew members, Annie worked her way up to the one who was busiest and most distracted. This was another beautiful tall blonde, obviously enamored with the handsome captain. Holding the two passes together as if they were one, Annie handed them to this girl.

In a few moments the crew would count the cards,

making sure that everyone was on board.

The cruise ship left the dock at 3:30. Glancing at her watch, Annie wondered about Robert. Where was he at that very moment? The moment that she was leaving. What was he doing? She wanted to picture him in all his stubborn, rude, selfish, horse-ass glory.

In another hour he would come to the dock, and he would realize he'd been left behind. She, however, wouldn't admit he wasn't on the ship until after the dinner hour.

She had seen no vehicles and no telephones in the village of Svirstroy. And the townspeople spoke no English. He might be stranded for several days, at least until another cruise ship came along.

It would be a mess.

And then, when at last he was rescued and back on board *The Felicity*, how would he behave? Would he act better? Maybe not. But he would have to wonder what she might do next. Now that he knew what she was capable of, he might be nervous. Certainly, he would be exhausted. Embarrassed. Humiliated. Well, good.

Blissfully, peacefully, Annie lay down in their cabin to take a nap before dinner. Closing her eyes, she made plans to find the Grosmans before the meal, and to sit with them. Of all the people on this trip that Robert detested, the Grosmans were her favorites.

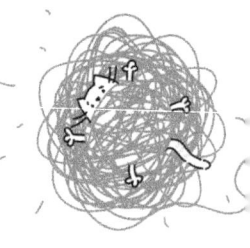

DESOLATION

In the summer of 1947, my father decided to move from the Texas Panhandle to the plains of South Dakota, where he bought a cattle ranch. Daddy had grown up as a farm boy during the Depression in East Texas, and he went to law school to make sure he wouldn't have to farm. But before long, he grew tired of being an attorney. He was weary of messy divorce cases, disillusioned by vicious readings of wills, sick of ranchers trespassing on each others' territory, and disgusted by clients who refused to pay their bills. So, Daddy found a ranch far away. Both my parents said it was an easy move; the only catastrophe was the smashing up of Mother's bicycle.

Upon reaching our new home, we immediately became celebrities. As my parents began renovating an old farmhouse, the locals came to welcome us and to see three foreign things: our indoor plumbing, Mother's baby grand piano, and our Negro hired help. The locals had heard of indoor plumbing, but grand pianos were foreign, and most had never seen black skin.

An only child, I was six years old. While the adults worked, I hid behind furniture and rolled-up carpet and played with a baby chick – a tiny fluff of yellow, alive and hopping about one day, then stone dead the next morning.

A neighbor gave us a gray-striped cat, along with her litter of half-grown kittens. They lived in the barn, and, after the chick died, the kittens became my playmates. I dressed them in doll clothes and put them in a doll buggy and pushed it over lumpy grass and gravel. They often tried to run away, but I was fast enough to pluck them from the ground and shove them back into the carriage.

I started school in an old white wooden building that had once been a church, with a bell in the steeple. Two grades were in each classroom. In the first grade I learned to read, to add and subtract, and to play jacks.

For much of the time, my pretty mother went silent. She had been a Dallas debutante and a sorority girl. Late one night when I couldn't sleep, I heard her tell my dad that living on a lonesome ranch was not her cup of tea. We never drank tea, so I thought she was absurd.

Absurd was one of Mother's favorite words. And *ridiculous* and also *unforgiveable.*

Meanwhile, the kittens flourished.

For Christmas I asked for a chameleon, that I'd seen advertized in a magazine. It was a tiny green thing and it came in the mail. I hid behind a skirted bed and played with it. But as the days went by, the lizard slowly turned brown, then shriveled and died. Mother and I wrapped it in a page from *Life Magazine* and asked Daddy to bury it. He refused to perform its funeral service and dumped it in the trash.

Will and Joe, the Negroes, were homesick, so during the Christmas holidays I went with Daddy to drive them back to Texas. We left early one morning and traveled for two days and one night, stopping only to buy food and gas. At mealtime, Daddy went into the restaurants and made arrangements for the Negroes to eat outside, behind the kitchen. After finishing our meal, Daddy drove around to the back of the restaurant, where they would be waiting. We never stopped at a motel, called "tourist courts" back then. The three men took turns sleeping and driving.

"No need to stop," Daddy said. "Let's just keep on trucking."

Will and Joe agreed.

After we delivered the men to their homes, it took three hard days of driving to get back to the ranch. Along the way, Daddy and I spent two nights in motels. During the day, I watched my father concentrate on the road ahead, holding a bottle of Wild Turkey between his knees. We seldom spoke. Sitting in the front seat with Daddy, I stared out at the bright blue sky and barren fields for hours.

One day, after we returned, Daddy and I counted nineteen cats. "Too many," he said.

The winter of '48 was brutal. Cowboys would come and go with warnings about horrendous blizzards. Sometimes the mounds and hillocks of snow were a dazzling, blinding white. Other times, the sky was as grey as a tombstone, the land as barren as a moonscape. School was canceled, stores were closed, and people kept their kids inside. Even our cats, that lived in the barn, began to disappear.

Stories circulated about how many cattle died. Lying on their backs, legs and feet pointed upward, they were stiffly frozen. Starved hoofed statues in fields of white.

Mother decided to teach me to play the piano. We started out with "Sailor's Hornpipe," a very complicated piece. Her long elegant fingers skittered over the keyboard with amazing speed. When my short fingers tried to follow her example, they fumbled miserably.

"You are just like your daddy," she said, grabbing my wrists. "No musical ability at all."

The winter slowly continued: one gray day after another.

Mother took to wearing her long purple robe all day. She smoked Lucky Strikes and stared out the living room window, watching occasional vehicles pass by on the highway.

"I'm sad today," she once told me. "You don't remember this, but you used to have a baby brother."

When spring finally came, Mother was so relieved she decided we should start going to church. In the small town 20 miles away, there were only two churches– Catholic and Lutheran.

"I could never be a Catholic," Mother said. "They'll damn you straight to hell every minute."

Near the pulpit in the Lutheran Church there was a large painting of a fair, blond Jesus, patiently knocking on a wooden door. Our Sunday school teacher said, "Notice that there's no door knob. That means the door can only be opened from the inside. You must open the door of your heart to let Jesus in. He won't come in uninvited."

I stared at the painting and waited for beautiful sweet Jesus to knock on my heart. But I felt nothing. Finally, I realized that I must be so far on my way to hell that I couldn't feel him knocking.

One night at supper my mother spoke. "I'm slowly dying here."

Not long after that, in early spring, a line of circus trucks came creeping over the horizon. They had almost reached the front of our house when one of them toppled over. Mother shed her purple robe, put on a jacket and a pair of corduroy slacks and went out to see if she could help.

The circus troupe stayed for three days, waiting for a new part for the broken truck. All the while my mother cooked – stews, chili, beans and lots of potatoes.

She wrung the necks of five scrawny chickens and fried them Southern style. She climbed down into the cellar and brought up every jar of canned fruit and vegetable we owned.

They put the circus animals in the barn and corral and the performers in our house and the bunkhouse. Mother gave my bedroom to trapeze artists from China, who spoke very little English. I slept downstairs on a pallet in Mother and Daddy 's room.

I'd never seen my mother so animated.

The circus troupe was a raucous bunch – loud,

colorful, and fun. I could tell Mother liked the ringmaster best of all. His name was Jack, and he was a strong, busy, red-headed man. One night Mother played "Stardust," and Jack sang. His voice was so gorgeous I fell in love with him. Mother had lots of sheet music, and soon all the performers got into the act and began to sing and dance.

Then, one afternoon when the bus dropped me off from school, the circus trucks were gone. To repay us for our hospitality, the performers left big piles of trash and loads of stinking manure.

On the kitchen table, Mother had left a note for Daddy. He never told me what it said.

At the end of the following summer, Daddy took me back to Texas to live with his parents. I didn't like them much. It was my grandmother who told me that Daddy had shot the cats.

"Had to do it," she said, "else they would've starved to death."

I lived with Daddy's parents until I finished high school. Eleven long years, except for summers, which I spent with him. He stayed on the ranch for the rest of his life.

Occasionally, Mother sent me a Christmas or a birthday gift from places I'd never heard of. But I never saw her again.

And I never learned to play the piano. But I did go to college, and I became a second-grade teacher. I never married, never had my own children, but I loved my students desperately.

These memories, which sometimes nearly knock me down with a rush, are events that happened over seventy years ago. Although my doctors tell me otherwise, I believe that somehow, I drove my mother away. Jesus never knocked on the door to my heart. But for comfort, I still have my mother's purple robe.

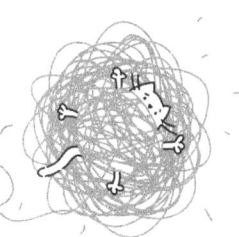

THE OLD RUGGED CROSS

"Look at that!" Harry Morrison pointed to the thermometer above the windshield in the SUV. "Hell, it's hotter than a witch's teat!"

"That's not right," said his wife, Cynthia. "The saying is '*cold*er than a witch's teat,' not *hotter*. A witch's teat would be cold."

"For God's sake! You know what I mean." The thermometer read one hundred and twelve degrees.

"Lordy!" Cynthia said. "We've got the AC going full blast." Although her stomach was held tight by her seatbelt, she turned to look around. "You kids OK?"

"I think they're asleep," her husband said.

"Poor babies. They've had a rough weekend."

"They aren't the only ones," Harry said. "I'm so tired I could eat a horse."

"Good grief, Harry."

"Ha! I knew that would get your goat! Seriously, for the next show we shouldn't take four kids, maybe only two. It's hard to manage them."

"No, we have to take four! And maybe some of the others! I wouldn't dream of leaving Marilyn or Robert

Downy Junior, Junior or Willy Shakes or The Divine Bette Mid behind. Besides, they've won ribbons. Are you out of your mind?"

Traveling south on I-44 from St. Louis to Oklahoma City, the Morrisons evaluated recent wins at the regional cat show. They whizzed along, surrounded by late weekend summer traffic.

"Oughta be a law against all these damned trucks on the road," Harry said. "Especially on Sunday."

Grumbling, he drove, while Cynthia fell into a broken chicken neck sleep.

A long bridge stretched ahead, with a railing on Cynthia's side, and a deep ditch below. On Harry's left, an eighteen-wheeler pulled close, the driver scowling and honking. On the pavement ahead of the Morrisons sat a large plastic jug.

"I can't miss it!" Harry yelled. And he didn't. "Oh, God! It's probably full of gasoline!"

The jug, caught by the car's undercarriage, made a *whooshing* sound, then a *thump-a-thump, thump-a-thump* while Harry pulled the SUV past the railing, to the wide gravel shoulder.

"Get out!" he screamed.

"What about the kids?" Cynthia was fully awake now.

"Oh, goddamnit!" Harry opened the backdoor and pulled out mammoth cages, tossing them to the ground. One by one, Cynthia ran with the cages to the ditch.

But the car didn't explode.

"It isn't even spewing," said Cynthia.

With vehicles zooming by at top speed, Harry got down on his knees and looked under the car.

"That jug hit the oil filter. We're losing oil." He climbed into the driver's seat and turned the key. The engine clanged and the oil warning light came on.

"I'll have to call the Auto Club," he said.

"Tell them to hurry," Cynthia told him. "These kids'll get so hot they might die."

After making the call, Cynthia and Harry stood beside the road. Dried brown grass and cockleburs waved with the fierce wind caused by passing automobiles. The yellow sky burned down, and no one stopped to help.

Inside the cages, the cats cried and panted. Cynthia, also panting, poured cool water from an ice chest and dropped wet rags into the animal's cages. On her knees, she encouraged each one.

"Lick the rag, honey, or you'll get dehydrated."

Harry, balding, tall and thin, with a middle-aged paunch that stretched the front of his blue knit shirt, stood with his thumbs in the back pockets of his khaki shorts, watching the traffic. "You'd think one of these sons of bitches would stop and give a traveler some aid," he said.

Cynthia said, "If I don't get to a bathroom soon, I may just die."

"Oh, for God's sake," her husband said.

"Nobody's going to stop and help us, Harry, and I've got a serious problem!"

She stacked the cat cages, two deep, in an L. The cats yowled. "Come stand in this space, Harry. And watch the road."

Harry obeyed. In the heat, Cynthia's urine sizzled as it hit the ground.

"That's much better," she announced, buttoning her shorts. She watched vehicles race by. Like her husband, she wore khaki shorts, but with an extra-large muumuu blouse. Her hair was a gray papery wasp's nest.

Thirty minutes later the wrecker appeared. The driver jumped out of the cab. He was a small young man wearing greasy jeans and t-shirt and a red cap turned backwards. His stringy hair was long and blond.

"My name's Joe," he said. You folks got trouble?"

"Our savior," said Cynthia.

"I'll tow your car into town," he told them, after surveying the damage caused by the empty plastic jug. "You can ride with me in the cab."

"What about our cats?" asked Cynthia.

"What about them?"

"We'll have to take them in the cab. They can't ride in the hot car."

"Lady, I ain't got no room for them cats!" the mechanic answered. "Besides, I'm allergic!"

"I'm not leaving my babies! If your cab is air-conditioned, we're all riding with you!"

"There ain't no room!"

"We'll put two in each cage, and Harry and I will each hold a cage on our lap."

"I'm allergic!"

"You'll get over it!" Crouching on the ground, Cynthia pulled out a blue-eyed white Persian named Marilyn

Munro and stuffed her into the cage occupied by Grand prize winner Maine Coon Robert Downy Junior, Junior.

She shouted, "Harry, help me!" But Harry was wondering how much of a tip would persuade Joe to cooperate. Pulling his billfold out of his hip pocket, he handed the mechanic a twenty, then another, then a ten. Then one more twenty.

Cynthia stuffed gigantic Maine Coon Willy Shakes into the cage with a yellow Persian with amber eyes, The Divine Bett Mid.

"Them is some kind of cats," Joe said. "More like mountain lions."

"They're our best show cats," Cynthia said. "Worth over $3000 each. Besides our house and car, they're our biggest investment. We have seven more show cats at home."

"Well, I'll be dad burned," said Joe, placing the money in his billfold and then into his back pocket.

"You carry these cages," Cynthia told the men. "They each weigh over fifty pounds."

She climbed into the cab, and Harry put a cage on her lap. Then he climbed in, and Joe handed him the other one. They started off.

"Where are we headed?" asked Harry.

"Veralmar, Oklahoma," Joe said.

"Isn't there a mental institution in Veralmar?" Cynthia asked.

"Yes, but them people don't bother us none."

In the front seat between the two men, Cynthia was

glad she'd worn shorts. Otherwise she'd have burned up by now. But she wasn't glad that lately she'd gained so much weight. She could feel Joe's hip next to hers on the left, and Harry's on the right. She was wider than either of the men, maybe wider than both combined.

She blamed the cat shows for her weight gain. When she and Harry entered the kids in a show, she ate continually. Nibble, nibble, to calm her nerves. Some people drank, some smoked, some talked incessantly, but Cynthia ate. That's how stressful the competition was. Enough to make her gain almost a hundred pounds. She was so heavy she refused to get on the scales, couldn't stand the bad news.

And now she was wedged in between two men, her bottom and legs sweating like a pen of pigs, despite the air-conditioner turned on High. In too tight shorts, her wet legs went to sleep under the heavy, crying cats. Hot, crowded, scared, miserable. When they stopped screaming, they panted. They would probably have heatstroke and fall over dead any minute.

"Mister, if it's going to be very much farther, we'll need to stop and give the kids some water," Cynthia said.

He didn't answer, and she turned to look at his profile. Tears streamed down his cheek. Sniffing, he wiped his nose and eyes with the backs of his wrists. Cat hair flew around inside the cab. Coming from the cages and held aloft by the air-conditioner, it swirled about. Before long, Joe's cab, like their SUV, would be lined with a heavy layer of fur.

Joe sneezed. "I can't hardly breathe," he said, as he reached over to direct a vent toward his face.

"*You* need a drink of water," Cynthia said, but he ignored her.

Joe turned on the radio, dialing to a Christian station as a deep baritone voice sang,

"On a hill far away
Stood an old rugged cross
The emblem of suff'ring and pain."

"I'm sorry about your allergies. When we get to town, I'll buy you some Benadryl," Cynthia said.

Joe ignored her. Between sneezes he sang along with the radio:

"*And I'll cling to the old rugged cross*
'Til at last I inherit a crown."

Joe drove through Veralmar, a brown dusty village, steaming in the yellow heat, to its outskirts. Then he turned into a narrow gravel drive. There, amid several disassembled cars and trucks, a house-trailer stood next to a tin building with a sign saying, *Wilsons' Tow Truck Garage*. He pulled his tow truck up next to the trailer, where an old brown and white hound watched from the open screened-in door.

"I'll leave you folks here," he said, "while I go back to town for an oil filter. I'll take my car over there." He pointed to a green 1987 Ford.

"Leave us here? Abandon us?" asked Cynthia.

"I'll be back in ten minutes. Fifteen at the most."

"Why didn't we stop in town?" Harry asked.

"No place to park," Joe said, "Listen, if ya'll are afraid I won't be back, one of you can ride along. But no cats."

"I'm not staying here by myself!" Cynthia said. "And I'm not leaving the children."

"Go on," Harry told Joe. "Just try to hurry, will you?"

Cynthia and Harry took the cats out of their cages. The animals wore leashes, but despite the heat, they pulled and strained, trying to run away. But Harry held them tight. Robert Downy Junior, Junior pulled on his collar and leash so hard he nearly choked. He found shade under the SUV.

Cynthia poured water from the ice cooler into a large dish. She tried wringing a wet rag over the other three cats' heads, but they hissed and spit at her. All the while the hound dog, looking through the trailer's screen door, sounded mournful and throaty.

"We've done all we can to cool them off," Cynthia said. "Why did this day turn out so rotten?"

"Everything will be all right," Harry said, as they sat down in front of the trailer, and he patted her leg. *Years ago*, she thought, *his hand was huge on my leg. Now it looks tiny. My, how I have grown.*

They rested together on the stoop of the faded blue trailer house, in the shade, the ragged screen separating them from the hound. They each held two leashes. Cynthia dozed, then shook herself. She looked at Harry, who was snoring. It wouldn't do for them to go to sleep and accidentally let go, so she tightened her hold and nudged Harry awake.

She thought she heard a sound coming from inside the trailer. She whispered to Harry, "Someone's there."

Harry didn't hear her, so she repeated, "Someone's inside the trailer! I can feel it!"

He turned and peered inside. "It's just the old dog."

"Shhh! Keep your voice down! Let's get away from here!" She pulled herself up from the stoop and moved toward her drooling darlings.

"Anybody in there?" Harry knocked on the screen. The hound sat on its launches and moaned. "See, I told you," Harry said, sitting back down on the stoop. "Nobody's in there but the dog."

Joe returned. "Told you it wouldn't take me no time," he said. "I'll have you on your way pretty quick."

He climbed into the SUV and drove it onto the lift. After jumping out, he raised the car and stood underneath.

"I thought the trouble was under the hood," said Cynthia.

"No Ma'am! The trouble is the oil filter, right here," he said.

While he worked, Joe hummed "The Old Rugged Cross." Soon he stood back, lowered the car, got in on the driver's side and started the engine. Getting out again, he said, "Well, folks, you can be on your way."

"You're the best mechanic ever," Cynthia said, putting Marilyn into her cage.

"I never saw anything like it. Thank you, sir!" Harry said to the mechanic. "You saved the day!"

"And our lives," said Cynthia. "We're truly grateful."

She snapped a cage shut.

"You people wait a minute!"

Cynthia, Harry, Joe and the cats looked toward the voice. A pale young man in black jeans and white t-shirt stood inside the trailer door. Stepping around the dog, he opened the screen and moved down to the stoop. His eyes were a bright and piercing blue.

"Don't nobody move or make a sound. Everything's OK," he said, walking toward them. He carried a gun.

"Please don't hurt us. I've got a little money," Harry said.

"What are *you* doing here?" Joe asked the stranger. "When did you get out?"

"I didn't." The man laughed. Turning to Harry, he said, "I know you got money. And I'll get it. Just give me the car keys now." He grabbed the ring from Harry. Cynthia finished putting Willy Shakes into his cage and snapped the door shut. She held onto the leash of Robert Downy Junior, Junior.

"Here, take our money. Just let us leave," Harry said, reaching for his billfold.

"I said, don't nobody move." The stranger pointed the gun at Harry's chin.

Cynthia thought that the man's eyes looked like sharp blue rocks.

"Before you people come, I was practicing. Let me show you what I can do with this." he said. He knelt down, aimed the gun at Robert Downey Junior, Junior, who watched him intently. The stranger pulled the trigger, the cat's body twitched violently, and then it lay still.

Cynthia held tight to the cat's leash.

"Who the hell is this?" Harry asked, looking at Joe.

"Shut up!" the stranger said. "Don't say a word."

"Oh, my baby, baby, baby!" Cynthia sobbed, kneeling over the cat.

"Don't move!" the man told her. He pointed the gun at Harry. "Give me your cell phone." He turned to Joe. "Your phone inside the trailer don't work no more." Then, to Harry, "Now help me carry them cats over the other side of that trailer. I can't stand to see nothing caged up."

With his shoulders slumping, Harry picked up Marilyn Munro and Willy Shakes in their cages. The stranger lifted the other one. He carried The Divine Miss Bette's cage with the wire door to the rear. Miss Bette looked at Cynthia and howled.

"He's taking you for a nice walk, honey. Don't worry," Cynthia told Miss Bette.

"Get moving," the man said to Harry.

"Are you going to let them loose?" Cynthia asked. "Please let them go!"

The stranger turned to Cynthia and Joe. "Get inside the trailer and shut the door. If you step outside, I'll shoot you both."

They went inside the stifling trailer house. She couldn't stop crying. "Oh, please, please, let them go."

She looked at the tiny windows, only large enough for a cat to crawl through, and cried harder.

In a few minutes, she heard three shots, then a fourth.

She turned around and saw Joe squirming through a narrow side window. He dropped out of sight, so she stumbled to the window and, looking out, watched him run to the Ford. He jumped in and started the car.

"Take me too," she screamed, rushing from the trailer, across the driveway, to the car. Joe reached across to open her door. But another shot rang out, and his head fell forward, hitting the steering wheel. The motor died.

Cynthia couldn't hear her own sobs or her breathing. She wanted to run but couldn't move. She watched the stranger approach and grab her arm, sinking his fingers deep into the flesh.

How big my arm has grown, she thought. How fat, yet how helpless. "What are you going to do with me?"

"Don't worry," he said and laughed. "I ain't going to rape you. I ain't that desperate. I don't hook up with old fat girls."

"Nor would I want you to," she said.

"What's that supposed to mean?" His eyebrows shot up and his fingers dug deeper.

"I mean you're a piece of shit. You've shot my husband and my cats, and you can go straight to hell."

"I imagine I will, lady. I'll do that."

"I'm serious," Cynthia wasn't crying any more. "Your sorry soul will burn in hell forever. In the meantime, you can go ahead and shoot me. Put me out of my misery. You sociopath."

"Funny, that's what my doctors said."

"Funny, but that's no excuse."

"I didn't mean for things to get so out of hand. I left the hospital just this morning." He loosened his hold.

"How did you know Joe?"

"From ninth grade. I found the gun in his trailer."

"And you wanted to use it."

"Oh, yeah."

"So, you've killed two good men and four lovely cats. What a day you've had. You bastard."

"That's probably true. The bastard part." He let go of her arm.

"That's no excuse, either. So, shoot me and get it over with. Then get to running. See who else you can kill along the way. And burn in hell." She looked at him. "What are you waiting for? Listen, I'm going over behind the trailer to say goodbye to my husband. Shoot me any time."

"I got only one bullet left."

"That's all you need."

Cynthia made her way around the trailer, wading through tall dry grass. She sank to her knees next to Harry, who lay on his right side, shot through his left temple. Then she looked at her babies, trapped and splattered in their cages. The field was still and quiet. She thought she could hear tiny insect wings as she waited for the stranger.

She heard a shot behind her.

She hoped he hadn't killed himself. Whatever would she do with three dead men and four dead cats?

After a while, she inched back to the trailer. There she found the stranger sprawled out on the stoop, his eyes and the top of his head a mass of crimson blood and bone.

Beside him was Harry's cell phone. She reached over the dead man to get it.

Hearing a moan from the mechanic's automobile, she realized that Joe was still alive. Poor Joe, shot because of her cowardice and her screams. She staggered to him. But the sounds weren't Joe's. Instead, she found the hound, groveling in the hot dirt on the driver's side of the car.

Cynthia collapsed beside the dog and began punching 9-1-1, 9-1-1, 9-1-1.

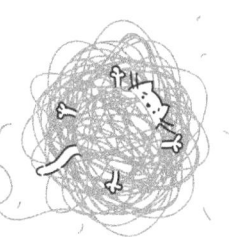

ON TOP OF OLD SMOKEY

Maribeth Warner wanted to write a country-western love song. Composing wailing music was her desperate desire, but she didn't know how to begin. In her spare time, she sat at the old upright piano her grandmother had given her, plunking the keys, scrambling for words. A demanding job, it left her depleted.

Her first effort was a ballad entitled "Swinging in the Clouds of Love." With a waltzing romantic melody suited for violins, it reminded her of movie musicals of the 50's. She thought the lyrics were wonderful:

Swinging in the clouds of love,
Never coming down to earth.
The earth is dusty.
The clouds are gay.
I shall come down to earth another day.

Maribeth took the song to Dr. Henry Lunt, professor of music at the college where her husband, George, had taught history for years.

"Tell me the truth, Henry," Maribeth said. "Don't

spare my feelings."

"This doesn't sound like a country-western song. Too dreamy, and the lyrics aren't homespun. I'd avoid the word 'gay,' if I were you."

"Oh, for heaven's sake," she said. "What words can I use?"

"I don't know what's popular, but country-western songwriters use a lot of clichés. Sometimes the songs tell a story. With twang and bang. But country music isn't my field of expertise. If you want to learn about English and French madrigals, I can help you."

Maribeth tried again. She wrote her next song about a hard-working waitress, who was sent to prison for stealing from the café cash register. This woman became a criminal to buy school supplies for her seven children, because her husband was too shiftless to hold a job. Maribeth got this material from the local newspaper, as well as from gossip at the beauty shop.

Her real-life model was Tammy Sue Parsons, who went to jail for robbing the restaurant where she worked. Tammy Sue served her time, while her lazy husband stayed home with the kids. Maribeth sympathized with the waitress, wanting to call attention to the plight of poor women with sorry husbands everywhere. She entitled this song, "When I Got Out of Prison, I Expected a Yellow Ribbon, but All I Got Was Empty Beer Cans and Piles of Dirty Clothes."

When Maribeth took this music to Dr. Lunt, he asked, "Why don't you try writing fiction? I'm not sure that you can put actual people into songs without getting into legal difficulties. Why don't you get a job in journalism?"

"Because I'm retired, Henry. I don't want a job. I want a lucrative hobby."

"Well, what do I know? After all, country-western music isn't my area. But I'd be glad help you compose a madrigal."

Leaving the college campus, Maribeth decided not to bother Henry Lunt again. She also wondered if he were a gay misogynist. *Misogynist* was a wonderful word, she thought, but probably not suitable for a CW love song.

Maribeth and her husband, George, retired from their jobs exactly one year apart. She was the first to leave the work force, having been employed by the City Water and Light Company as secretary/clerk for years. Adjusting to retirement, she sorted through closets, hauled carloads of junk to Goodwill, and made her grown children come get their clutter. While cleaning out cabinets, she listened to country stations in Lubbock, Amarillo, and Oklahoma City. As she worked, she sang along with the stars. That's when she decided to become a songwriter.

When the house was in order, Maribeth had Grandma's piano tuned, and she bought clean blank paper, lined for musical scores. Then she began.

Soon after Maribeth began composing, George announced he was taking early retirement. Maribeth's face fell. "Oh, George, you won't be happy!" she exclaimed. "You won't like staying home all day!"

"Of course, I will," he answered. "I have hobbies of my own."

Maribeth scolded herself. Of course, George should be allowed to retire. Hadn't he worked hard for over forty years — giving lectures, presenting papers, writing articles, grading tests, and attending committee meetings? What was the matter with her?

Maribeth awoke that night, feeling guilty for not encouraging George. She moved over to him and started nibbling on his ear. She put her hand under the elastic waistband of his polar bear pajamas. But George was sleeping so soundly he didn't respond.

"Oh, why bother? I have a better idea." Quietly, she went into the living room and composed "I Love to Hear a Good Man Snore."

🐾 🐾 🐾

Shortly after George retired, Maribeth's elderly uncle in the Texas Panhandle died, and, as a result, Maribeth inherited her grandmother's house — a farmhouse large and lovely. Maribeth was eager to move there.

"We'll sell our house, move to Grandma's, and save a ton of money, George," she insisted, and he agreed.

They moved in early summer. Shortly after getting their home in order, Maribeth resumed her songwriting and wrote the tune, "Give Me Land Lots of Land in the Homey Land of Hud." She sent it to Dr. Lunt, who replied almost immediately, "Maribeth, those youngsters in the country-western field will have no idea who Hud is."

Frustrated and disappointed, Maribeth read the letter.

She vowed once more not to bother Henry Lunt again. What to do? He was her only contact with the music world, and he was worthless! She *must* manage to meet a CW star or get an agent. But how would she begin? "I haven't a clue," she told herself and then wondered if "I Haven't a Clue" would make a good title of a song.

At that moment George came into the kitchen. He briefly looked through the mail and then announced he was ready to begin his new hobby.

"Since you've never had a hobby in your life, George, what do you plan to do?"

"I want to study the famous American military battles and then visit the battlefields. I'll start by ordering a few miniature soldiers to set up, to help me visualize the major historic confrontations."

George joined a national historic battle club and communicated with other history buffs over the internet. Soon, boxes of miniature soldiers arrived. Maribeth had never seen George so excited as when he opened a new box of militiamen. In a few weeks, George was walking from room to room with drafting paper and a measuring tape. Then he hired a local carpenter to build tables for historical re-creations.

Within six months George took over Maribeth's ancestral home. Grandma's parlor was dedicated to the Civil War and contained four large dioramas, all of which held a multitude of miniatures re-creating battles.

"Do you know what the Union Army officers did to deserters?" George asked Maribeth. "Sometimes they killed them, but usually they tortured them in horrible ways. Most often they used hot branding irons with the letter *D* and branded their buttocks or their faces. Union doctors were forced to brand the prisoners. Didn't know that, did you?"

George told Maribeth more than she had ever wanted to know about the battles and the soldiers.

"You're wearing me out with these details, George," Maribeth said one day. She went to her piano and composed "An Exhausted Woman Can't Love."

Each time a new shipment of soldiers arrived, Maribeth admonished, "Don't throw away those boxes, George. We may need them some day."

Next, George dedicated the large farmhouse den to the Revolutionary War. Stacking furniture against the wall, he brought in five new tables. British, colonial, French, and Spanish soldiers lined up in an assortment of battle scenes.

"The Spanish were essential allies, and helped the Colonists win the Revolution," George remarked to Maribeth. "Didn't know that, did you?"

Shaking her head, she retreated to the piano. She wanted to write a country-western war song but couldn't decide how to begin. She played, "When Johnny Comes Marching Home Again," and sang,

When Johnny comes marching home again, hurrah, hurrah,

We'll give him a hearty welcome then, hurrah, hurrah —

"Wrong war! That song is from the wrong war!"

shouted George from the den. "That was written by Patrick Gilmore in 1863. He was the bandmaster of the Union Army during the Civil War. Didn't know that, did you?"

Maribeth sat at the piano, looking at her hands. Then she pounded on the keys, playing the tune "Chicago." She thought of Old Blue Eyes singing her lyrics, and she laughed as she sang,

Retirement! Retirement!
It's a wonderful thing!
Retirement! Retirement!
It just makes me sing!

George didn't get the joke. To send him another message, Maribeth started playing from her grandmother's hymnal. "Rock of Ages" as slowly as a funeral dirge. Then "Amazing Grace." She wanted to shout, "This song was written by the captain of a slave ship after he renounced his sinful ways. Didn't know that, did you, George!" But of course, George *did* know that. George knew *everything*.

She remembered years ago, at a faculty cocktail party she had asked Dr. Barkley, distinguished professor of veterinary medicine, an important question.

"Ever since I was a little girl, I've wondered what kind of horse Old Smokey was."

Dr. Barkley looked blank.

"From the song 'On Top of Old Smokey.' What kind

of horse was the singer riding?"

Dr. Barkley smiled at her. "I don't remember the song. Sing a few bars to me."

Maribeth was happy to perform:

On top of Old Smokey
All covered with snow,
I lost my true lover
For courtin' too slow.

George was standing nearby. "Old Smokey wasn't a horse! Old Smokey is a *mountain*. You know— the Smokey Mountains! What an idiot!" he laughed.

Everybody laughed. Maribeth managed to smile brightly, "Oh, of course, how silly of me."

🐾 🐾 🐾

Their family came for Christmas. Everyone had to negotiate around the battle tables. The children occasionally knocked over a soldier or two. "Please, Grandpa, can't we play with them?" they asked.

"Of course not," he replied. "But let me describe this battle to you."

The children returned to their homes the day after Christmas. "I wish they'd been able to stay longer," said Maribeth.

"Those damned kids are spoiled and destructive," George replied.

She went to the piano and composed "Grandpa is a Grumpy Old Man."

For World War II George took over two rooms upstairs. The day he reconstructed D Day was emotional. He recreated the beaches of Normandy with diorama materials, along with blue construction paper, glass and sand. Maribeth heard him weeping while making sounds of explosions and gunfire and knocking down the Allied soldiers. She went to the door of the room in which he was working.

"George, you're taking this too seriously. A hobby should be fun."

"Leave me alone," he sobbed. "I *am* having fun."

Maribeth went downstairs and played, "Praise the Lord and Pass the Ammunition."

Next, George took a corner of the kitchen for his workshop. He set up a long table and decorated the unpainted militiamen now arriving daily. Patiently, he explained each step of his endeavors to Maribeth.

"It's nice you're interested in this stuff, George, but country-western music is where the money is," she told him.

Maribeth decided to take Dr. Lund's advice and write a song consisting of familiar sayings, so she ordered a book of clichés from Barnes and Noble. When the book arrived, she sat quickly composed a tune:

"You can catch more flies with honey than vinegar,"

is what some people say.
Honest to goodness they do.
Make no bones about it, that don't make a lick of sense, and if I have my way
To mine own self, I will be true.

One day while Maribeth listened to the radio, she discovered that an ex-student of her husband's had recently been hired as a disc jockey for one of the country-western stations in Amarillo. Jeff Tolliver. Immediately, she called the station and invited him to come for dinner the following week.

On the next Sunday, Jeff arrived at 12:30. He was tall, handsome and very hungry. Maribeth served lunch almost immediately, for she wanted to waste no time in asking his advice. She had prepared a roast beef, mashed potato medley. While they ate, George explained how he and Maribeth wound up out in the boondocks.

"Yes," Maribeth added, "Just as we retired, we inherited this house. Wasn't that a co-inky-dink?"

Maribeth had arranged her songs on top of the piano. While serving apple pie *a la mode*, she told Jeff about her problems, and asked, "Would you be willing to take a teensy-weensy look at my songs?"

"Of course, I will." He cut his pie.

"If you think I have potential, could you please help me get in touch with Reba McIntyre or Garth Brooks?"

"I don't know them," he said. "But I'd love to hear your music."

"What about Toby Keith? I need his help with my lyrics."

"Don't know him either. Sorry."

"Before you get started," George said, turning to their guest, "I want you to look at my model battlefields."

While Maribeth cleaned up the kitchen, the disc jockey and George retreated. Later, despite occasional hints and nudges from Maribeth, they spent two hours talking about the models and battles. Finally, Jeff announced he must leave.

"So soon?" asked Maribeth. "But I haven't shared my music with you yet!" She hoped her panic didn't show.

"Maybe some other time," he smiled. "I have to get back for a date."

"Next time please bring your girlfriend with you," she said, walking him to the door.

"I'd like that," he answered, "but *she* wouldn't. If she came, she wouldn't eat. She hardly ever eats anything."

After Jeff left, Maribeth sat on the living room sofa, looking at her hands. In a little while, George descended from Normandy and said, "I think that went very well, don't you?"

"Oh, yes," she said. "It was peachy keen."

"By the way, what's for supper?"

"George, I'm longing for a weapon."

Maribeth went into a slump. For weeks she didn't go near her piano. "I'm in a blue funk," she told herself. "Maybe I'd feel better if I could write a song about it."

But she couldn't make herself move into the direction of the piano. "What's the use?" she muttered.

She remembered her cheerful grandmother, who could instantly snap a person out of feeling blue. On these occasions, Grandma's favorite saying was, "Stop your brooding, honey, and make new drapes."

🐾 🐾 🐾

Their fortieth anniversary was coming up in June. "Let's go to Vicksburg to celebrate," suggested George. "I've been reading about the Battle of Vicksburg."

"What state is Vicksburg in?" Maribeth asked.

"Mississippi. I wish you knew something about history or geography."

"But you know enough for both of us," she said. "And to what war are you referring?"

"The Civil War, of course."

"Oh, goody."

George made all the arrangements. Maribeth let him pack his own things, and she packed hers. "You'll enjoy this trip," he said. "Not only will we tour the battlefield, but also we'll visit antebellum homes and a famous old cemetery."

"Sounds grand."

"One day we'll drive over to Jackson," he continued. "That's where Eudora Welty — great writer of fiction — lived. You didn't know that, did you?"

"I really didn't know that, George."

"You don't sound enthusiastic."

"Oh, but I am thrilled to be going to Mississippi in the

middle of the summer. Stomping around some old battlefield and then trying to find an old dead writer's roots will be more fun than a barrelful of monkeys."

"You use too many clichés," he said, "And I don't appreciate your sarcasm."

"By the way," she told him, "For our next trip I'd like to go to Nashville. I want to see a show at the Grand Old Opry. I understand it's air-conditioned. I want to hear some of the famous performers there. I understand they're alive."

The morning after they arrived in Vicksburg, they drove to the battlefield, and George started making arrangements to hire a guide.

"Why don't we just buy a tape and listen to it as we drive through," suggested Maribeth. "Or better still, we could just whiz though the park with no commentary whatsoever."

"No," said her husband. "I want an intelligent human being here to talk to. These guides are very well educated."

George hired Tim Nation, red-faced and rotund. The two men sat in the front seat, and Maribeth sat in the back.

She thought Mr. Nation looked as if he had been physically stuffed with little papers containing facts about the Civil War. Within ten minutes of the tour, she concluded that he could win the Most Boring Human Being in the Entire Universe Contest. George would easily come in second.

They all climbed out of the car and stood on a bluff, looking down at the area where the Union soldiers had charged up the hill to attack the Confederates. History buff Tim Nation and history professor George Warner spoke with loud voices and waved their arms in the air as they imagined the battle.

Then Maribeth screamed. At first, she thought she'd been bitten by a snake. But when she looked down at her right foot, she saw it was covered with tiny swarming black specks.

"Fire ants!" yelled Nation. "Move out of the ant bed!" He pushed her gently. "Here, take your shoe off. Hold on to me. Get these damned things off!" Together he and Maribeth took off her sandal and beat the ants.

"Please help me back to the car," she said. She sat barefoot, with her right foot elevated for the rest of the tour, as Nation and George continued to discuss every aspect of the Civil War possible.

"I'd like to make a point," Maribeth said at the end of the tour. "You two gentlemen have talked all day about military strategy, while under your noses there's been the most remarkable example. The fire ants, I mean. They covered my entire foot, and then they attacked at the same moment. I was not aware of any individual ant sting. They all stung me at the same time.

"What are you saying?" asked Nation.

"They must have had a leader. Someone that signaled 'Sting!' so they all stung simultaneously! My right foot was standing in their territory; I was the enemy. They organized their army and attacked me."

"Don't mind her. She tends to babble," said George.

In the night, Maribeth awoke, her foot on fire. She limped to the hotel bathroom, turned on the light, and was amazed at the blisters that had formed. They were driving her crazy. She tried to awaken George, but with every shake he only snored louder, so she put on her robe and went down the hall for ice. It was two a.m.

She put the ice in the bathtub and then sat on the edge, numbing her foot, for more than an hour. At one point she lifted her foot and began counting the bites: forty-seven, not counting those on the bottom of her foot or between her toes, which she couldn't see.

Her foot was as hot as a fried turkey.

Maribeth was inspired to write a country western suffering song. She remembered Frankie Lane, strong-voiced and dramatic, singing "Mule Train!!" In her mind she could hear him sing,

Fire ants!
Softly hopping, causing hurt and pain.
Softly hop, never stop,
Quickly stinging a-long.

"I'm a wreck," she said. Total mental and physical wreck."

The next day they bought Benadryl, and she returned to their hotel room and slept, while George enjoyed their anniversary trip alone.

"There's one thing I'd like you to consider," she said to George during one of her waking moments. "If the fire ants were on the hill during the Civil War battles, couldn't they have influenced the outcome? Let's face it, the army with the most fire ant stings would lose the war."

George was quiet, so she continued. "Maybe the Yankees wouldn't have won the war at all if the Rebs hadn't been eaten up by fire ants. Are you listening to me, George? Answer me!"

"Your statement doesn't deserve an answer," he said. "Fire ants are a recent phenomenon, having just arrived in the United States from South America a few years ago. You didn't know that, did you?"

Maribeth put her head down on the pillow and went back to sleep.

Back home, Maribeth was spaced out for several days, but by the end of the week, her foot was healing, and she felt strong. One morning she sat drinking coffee. George had already climbed the stairs to do battle with the miniature soldiers. Hearing him scurrying around upstairs, she allowed a feeble desire to emerge. The more she thought about it, the more convinced she became. *She would like to live alone*.

She thought of her grandmother, fun loving and loud, a widow who had played the piano for the First Baptist

Church for fifty years. Music was such an important part of Grandma's life that every day she played and sang. Grandma named her old Angus cow Pearl Bailey, and every afternoon — even in bad weather — she raised the parlor window and sat down at the piano.

Won't you come home, Pearl Bailey?
Won't you come home?
I've cried the whole night long.
I'll do the cooking, honey,
I'll pay the rent —

Pearl Bailey always lumbered up to the parlor window, as Grandma finished the song. Then Grandma went outside to feed her.

"Grandma was a dreadful racist, but she knew how to have fun."

Maribeth climbed the stairs and entered the Normandy room. George bent over his miniatures, glasses perched on his head, concentrating.

"I need to talk with you, George."

"What is it? He reached for a soldier.

"Please listen to what I'm saying. I am going to leave you, George."

"May I ask why?" He began polishing the soldier with a soft rag.

"There's nothing about you I can stand."

"Oh, for a moment I thought I'd done something wrong."

"Everything about you is wrong, George."

"Absolutely everything?" He looked up at her.

"Everything. But some things are worse than others."

George stood straight. "Where will you go?"

"To Nashville, and I'll stay as long as I want. Eventually I'll come back here to live. In this house without you."

George was quiet for a long time. "What do you want?" he finally asked.

"I want you to throw away your soldiers. Every damned one."

"That's the reason you insisted we keep the boxes," he said.

"Whatever you say, George." Maribeth turned around and went to their bedroom. She took a suitcase down from a shelf in the closet and began packing.

🐾 🐾 🐾

Since the guest bedrooms were filled with militiamen, Maribeth spent the night on the sofa in the parlor. When she awoke, she could hear George moving around upstairs. Going to the garage, she saw that he'd removed the empty boxes. "So, he's throwing his soldiers away," she told herself. "Or at least he's pretending to do it."

She dressed, packed her car and then ate breakfast. Periodically George appeared, carrying boxes. He walked through the kitchen to the garage. From the kitchen window she watched as he piled the boxes in front of the house, next to the road.

She thought he made a great show of calling the

garbage collection department. He asked one of the officials there to send a truck to their home, outside city limits, to pick up his trash. A garbage truck would arrive within an hour.

"I'll believe it when I see it, George," she said. That would make a wonderful country-western song, she thought. She took out a piece of paper and scribbled:

I'll believe that you still love me when I see it in your eyes.

I can tell that you don't want me 'cause I hear it in your lies.

As she cleaned her kitchen, she heard the truck. Looking out the window, she saw the garbage boys grab the boxes and toss them up, oblivious to the treasures they were hauling away.

"They're gone," said George, standing behind her. "Are you satisfied?"

"Actually, no," she answered. "That isn't enough to make me want to stay."

Maribeth backed her car out of the driveway and headed toward town. She drove down the sad, dead Main Street, stopping at the ATM machine at the bank and withdrawing most of her savings. Then she headed to I-40 and, upon reaching the highway, she turned east, toward Oklahoma City, Little Rock, Memphis, and on. It would take her a long time to get to Nashville.

"Maybe I'll send George a postcard of the Grand Old Opry," she said. "But then again, maybe I won't."

She thought about her husband. She wondered if he were flagging down the garbage truck at that very moment, intent upon retrieving his soldiers before they reached the dump. Perhaps he was too late; perhaps he would have to go out there and search through other people's garbage to get to his own smashed boxes of militiamen. The whole ordeal could take him the better part of the day.

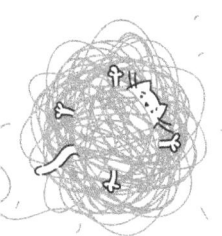

A DROWNING: SUMMER, 1944

I am standing on the floorboard of the backseat of my mother and father's black Chrysler, wearing a starched white pinafore with narrow lace trim on the ruffled straps. My dress has a long sash, which has come untied. This is my favorite sundress, mainly because the white material is covered with tiny bunches of purple violets. At my waist is a small bunch of artificial flowers. Tonight, they have been smushed flat by my leaning into the front seat. My white sandals are unbuckled, and my feet are covered with yellow West Texas sand. I drape my arms over the front seat and listen to my mother and my aunt talking. It's dark outside.

Behind me, on the backseat, my cousin Sarah lies sleeping. She is younger than I. I am eight and she is six. Sarah is missing all the excitement. I turn to watch her, thinking to myself it serves her right, to miss it all, to miss watching the men with no clothes on jumping into the water, to miss the drowning. I hope she sleeps through the whole thing.

I can't tell anybody this, but I hate Sarah. Hate hit me two weeks ago when I was walking into the living room.

I was standing behind Great Uncle Daniel's chair and I heard him say to her, "Sarah, you are as pretty as a princess. Yes, you could be a princess and your cousin Lucy could be your maid." Ever since that day I've hated pretty Sarah with her blue eyes and curly yellow hair. Oh, and I hate old Uncle Daniel, too.

Almost as much as I hate the Japs. And the Germans. I hear the grownups talk about them all the time. We all hate them and want the war to end. Mostly I want it to end so that Sarah's daddy will come home, and she and her mother will move out of our house forever. And I can have my room and peace and never have to worry about people thinking that I am so ugly I ought to be Sarah's maid. When I was six years old, my Aunt Beth taught me how to spell ugly.

Mother is behind the steering wheel, smoking Lucky Strikes. Aunt Beth is smoking also, and I can see their heads and shoulders outlined in the dark, with cigarettes glowing. If I am quiet, I will be able to hear everything they say. They seem frightened, and I have never before heard the soft choking sounds that come from them now.

Our car is parked among others facing the swimming pool, and the headlights are on. Beyond the area where the lights are shining, it is dark. But where the lights shine, we see men diving into the pool. I see my father, wearing only his underwear. He steps onto the diving board and dives into the black water. He does it again and again. He does not look like himself, with dripping wet hair and a pale, bare face. I do not remember ever seeing him without his glasses, except early mornings, when he first gets out of bed.

He is the only white man in the pool. The rest are colored, and they are looking for Miles Sloan's grandson.

Earlier this evening, we lay on quilts in the backyard. We ate strawberries and cream and talked about how the rich sweet berries had turned the thick cream to a lovely pink. We lay close to my daddy's rose garden and could breathe in the heavy scent of the blooms. "American Beauties are the best," Mother said, "because they have the loveliest fragrance."

When we finished our berries, we stretched out on our backs, counting the stars, and Daddy talked about the stars. He showed us the Big Dipper and the others, too. He told us about planets, and we listened to cicadas playing their soft music as he spoke. The sky was wide and black but twinkling, and it covered us like a blanket.

"There is nothing like a West Texas sky," Mother said, "to make you feel very, very small." Then she started singing,

> *Twinkle, twinkle little star.*
> *How I wonder what you are.*
> *Up above the world so high,*
> *Like a diamond in the sky.*

Suddenly, we heard a commotion from the backyard gate. Mother thought it was Daddy's old bird dog and got up to scold it. Then she called to Daddy, "There's been an accident! Miles is here and he needs you right now!"

Daddy went with Miles Sloan right then, and Mother and Aunt Beth put Sarah and me into the backseat of the car, and we drove to the city swimming pool as fast as we could.

Now the cars are taking turns shining headlights, so their batteries don't run down. An old colored man—I can't remember his name—comes to Mother's open window and says something. She switches off our lights, and the car next to us turns its lights on. I don't know how many cars there are, but they surround the swimming pool, and they belong to white people and colored people. They have white drivers and colored drivers. And I've never heard it so quiet.

"Why?" Aunt Beth asks. "Why did those boys want to go where they weren't allowed to go? They knew not to swim in the white folks' pool! Why on earth did they do it?"

"And after dark! Knowing that Willie couldn't swim! Why would they take the risk!" Mother's voice chokes.

"At least the others knew to come to get help! At least they tried to save Willie!" Aunt Beth adds.

"But they shouldn't have been here in the first place. What is the matter with those teenage colored boys!" Mother can't let it go.

"They probably just wanted to get in the water to cool off." Aunt Beth says.

Mother thinks for a long time. Then she says, "And they figured breaking into the white folks' pool would be fun."

They are silent, and I wonder what they are thinking. Then Aunt Beth speaks. "You know, those fellows may have been swimming in our pool at night for years."

"Well, it would serve us right if they did. I've never really thought about it before. But why don't they have a pool also?" Mother sounds angry. "That is so strange."

"What is?" asks Aunt Beth.

"That we've never thought about it until now." answers my mother.

After a while, Mother says, "I wonder why they put up with being treated this way."

"Well, they won't put up with it forever," answers Aunt Beth.

"No, I suppose not," Mother wipes her eyes with an old tea towel from the kitchen. "This is truly, truly lousy."

I watch my father pull himself up out of the deep end and head for the diving board again. Several other men are slowly walking back and forth across the shallow end.

My mother has told me that Daddy wanted to join the army, but they wouldn't take him on account of his poor eyesight. So, when his brothers, his cousins, and our neighbor men put on their uniforms and went to war, he stayed home. Now he looks after the families of his brothers, cousins and neighbors. But his main job is to work for the government. He watches over rationing stamps from Midland to El Paso.

There aren't many young white men left in our town and not many-colored ones either. So, Daddy takes care of a lot of things and a lot of people and, when there is trouble, they come for him. But we've never had trouble like this before tonight.

Mother puts her head down on the steering wheel. "Your daddy was one of the first men in the water, and he'll be the last one out."

The old man comes back to Mother's window. She turns her headlights on again. Then she and Aunt Beth light more cigarettes. The smoke swirls around our heads, and I inhale as deeply as I can. My arms still dangle between the women. Mother takes my hand, and I wrap my arms around her neck. She puts her cigarette in the car's ashtray, as she holds my arms and hugs them tightly.

"Oh, Lucy, you are a sweet girl. You are my dear, sweet little girl," she whispers.

Suddenly the men in the pool yell, "Light! Light! Give us more light!"

All the other cars turn their headlights on. We can see almost nothing, but the men are huddled at the deep end, both in and out of the water. They stay where they are for a long time.

Then we hear my father's voice. It sounds broken. "Blanket! Bring us a blanket! We need a blanket now!"

And we know they have found Willie Sloan.

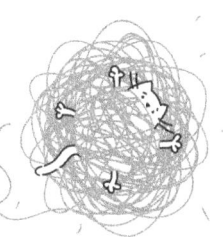

QUEENIE ADAMS:
Ladies in Waiting

Queenie Adams was surrounded by the things she loved. Dressed in a sky-blue silk gown and robe, she lay in her bed, silver head on plumped up pillows, and she breathed deeply. At the foot of her bed in his cage perched Dr. Dolittle, a green Amazon parrot, who hopped down from his swing and rummaged around on the floor of his cage for his afternoon snack. Occasionally Dr. Dolittle squawked, "Awwwk! Queenie! Kiss me quick!"

At Queenie's feet, her aged Persian cat, Griselda, lay in a gray mound. In cat years, Griselda was well over a hundred. She shifted and purred periodically; for decades her purpose in life had been to provide year-round warmth for Queenie's feet. Griselda slept almost twenty-four hours a day, and when she was awake, she was generally peevish.

Snuggled up by Queenie's side lay Moby Dick, a tiny white miniature poodle. He, too, was grizzled and old, and he had to be lifted up and down from the bed several times a day. Queenie herself was usually too weak to lift him, so that was one of the duties of her housekeeper. Years ago, in an effort to be ironic, Queenie had named the tiny poodle *Moby Dick*, and she was disappointed that no one else ever appreciated her attempt at humor.

Queenie Adams had just received a disconcerting telephone call, a call that presented what she considered to be a monumental problem. Berta Louise, Queenie's trusted friend and housekeeper, was quitting. After hearing the news, Queenie slowly returned the telephone to its cradle on the table beside her bed, then carefully picked up the clear plastic oxygen tubing, slipped it over her head, and reattached the nosepieces under her nostrils. She lay back and breathed deeply, hands folded over her chest, heart pounding heavily, like heavy feet marching in snow. She closed her eyes and gasped for breath through her mouth and began mentally re-organizing her important Final Project.

Her husband, cat, dog and parrot lived with Queenie in the only true mansion in the town of Clover, Texas. She had lived there almost all her life. She had married her high school sweetheart, the only son of the local banker, and she had moved to his family home—high on the only hill in that flat West Texas town. Shortly after the young couple married, Old Banker Adams, a widower, had allowed his son and daughter-in-law to take over the entire home, while he retreated to private quarters out behind the house, next to the tennis courts. Queenie and her husband, Rex, had lived in the mansion for over sixty-five years.

There they reared their family of four children and cared for old Mr. Adams until he died at the age of ninety-six; there they had entertained and taken in folks from all over Welles County, and there Queenie had set up her well-known costume shop. The costumes that she had constructed and collected were available to the townspeople for any occasion, and they were frequently borrowed for local parades, school plays, church Bible re-enactments, and theme parties. Every Halloween, Queenie, dressed as the Wicked Witch of the West, doled out costumes to anybody—rich or poor, large or small—who came to her door and asked for one. The only thing that she demanded in return was that the borrower brings the costume back "clean and in good condition."

Queenie's children had grown up and scattered like the wind, except for Luke, who had stayed in Clover and inherited the role of running the bank. Over the years, the Adams' children produced more children, and those grandchildren spent holidays and summer vacations with their grandparents— camping out in the backyard, sleeping in the treehouse, playing dress-up in the attic costume shop, acting out plays on the stage that Queenie had built for them, working with puppets in her puppet theater, and marching in their own family band around the swimming pool and the tennis courts, tooting their horns loud and strong, while Moby Dick pranced and jumped with excitement.

Because she secretly believed that all the traditional names her friends were being called by their grandchildren were insipid, she had named herself "Queenie" after her first grandchild was born. "If you are going to be called 'Granddaddy Rex,'" she had announced to her husband, "I'll be damned if I'm going to be called 'Granny' or 'Grandma.' I need a name with more pizzazz." So, from then on, she was known as "Queenie" and would answer to no other name.

Now, surrounded by those things that she loved, Queenie was depressed and disappointed. How had she become so old, so ill, so quickly? And how could Berta Louise leave her just on the eve of beginning her One Final Project? It was almost too much to bear. Feeble, shaky, and frail, she was sick of being hooked up to a machine that helped her breathe, and sick of carefully measuring out words to avoid depleting her strength. "Sick, just sick of the whole damned thing," she said, repeatedly.

She simply could not believe the bad news, but Berta Louise claimed to be in worse shape than Queenie, saying that she was about worn out. High blood pressure, bad back, rotten kidney (only one left, after the surgery), flat feet, diabetic, the list went on. Berta Louise's doctor had been adamant.

For years Queenie had planned for Berta Louise to care for her until she died. Some time ago she had given Berta Louise instructions about the black dress hanging in the closet for her funeral, as well as the faux pearl necklace and earrings and little golden cat pin, carefully placed in a box in her jewelry drawer.

So, Queenie Adams took this news bitterly. She looked at Dr. Dolittle, Moby Dick and Griselda and asked them all, "Can you see steam coming out of my ears?"

"Awwwwcckkkkk! Kiss me, Queenie!" responded the parrot.

That evening, when Luke made his nightly visit to his parents' home, Queenie wept at her loss of Berta Louise. "What hurts me most is that she did not even come to tell me," she cried. "Instead, she just called me from the doctor's office and quit! Just up and quit me! After all these years! And just after I had planned all this work that I simply must get done! Quit!"

"Qqqquuuiiitttt!" screamed Dr. Dolittle.

"Don't worry, Queenie," Luke said. "I will find someone to stay with you and help you with your daily routine—and your project."

So, Luke conferred with his father, letting him know that some changes were in store. "That is fine with me," announced old Mr. Adams. "Just tell whoever you hire to stay out of my way and to concentrate on taking care of your mother."

Within twenty-four hours Luke had found someone.

The first housekeeper/helper whom Luke found looked to be about thirteen years old. She wore long hair, jeans, and a short tight pink cotton sweater. "I can't believe that she'll know how to do anything," lamented Queenie, but Luke encouraged her. "Give Doretta a chance. She may surprise you."

Young, blonde, slender Doretta did surprise Queenie. Up at sunrise, she cooked, cleaned, laundered, scrubbed, ran errands, and told old Mr. Adams that she was going to box his ears if he did not eat his vegetables and clean his plate. She pampered, bathed and dressed Queenie, read stories from *The Reader's Digest* aloud, doled out the proper medications, and was generally cheerful and bright.

Doretta held out her arm to help Dr. Dolittle climb out of his cage, and she taught him to yell, "Beeyutiful Dorrrreettta!" She brushed tangles out of Griselda's fur and gave Moby Dick treats as they walked out on the lawn, morning and night.

Doretta also rearranged the furniture, re-hung the Adams' art collection, used the best silver and linens for every day, controlled Queenie's television watching and reading material, and, after working for the Adams for over a month, she became involved in paying household bills.

Queenie trusted Doretta completely, and was almost ready to propose beginning the Final Project when Luke asked her one evening, "Mother, when did you give Doretta a raise?" Luke had been sorting through the monthly bills and, concerned with what he found, he had examined the checkbook very thoroughly.

Queenie had given Doretta no raise, so that was the end of Doretta. Luke gave her two weeks' pay and told her to leave immediately. Crying, Doretta came in to tell Queenie good-bye. "I just wanted you to know that you are the first really old person that I ever almost liked," she sobbed.

The next person that Luke found to care for his mother was a large round brown woman of indeterminate race and age. She had wide features, a broad forehead, and she wore her salt and pepper straight hair twisted into a bun on top of her head. She wore an assortment of long smockish housedresses, which Queenie assumed were muumuus. Her name was Fatima.

"She is highly entertaining," said Queenie, when her daughter in Dallas asked her to describe Fatima over the telephone. "I don't know how well she cleans things, since I can't see too well, and she really is not much of a cook. But she has led an interesting life. She used to work for Liberace."

Fatima talked incessantly about her many adventures, and she moved about a room in slow undulating waves. Squinting, Queenie would watch Fatima move forward, and it would seem as if the entire wall, covered in wildly colorful wallpaper, were moving towards her.

"Her largeness in those dresses gives the most remarkable sensation," commented Queenie. "I could almost be afraid of her if I didn't like her so well."

Fatima had known all the Stars. Rarely did she and Queenie watch a soap opera or a game show that Fatima did not provide intimate information about whatever television personality they were watching. Rarely was a politician mentioned that Fatima could not gossip about.

"I would estimate that I am familiar with the families and the problems of ninety percent of the celebrities in America. I met them all through Liberace," she said.

Queenie listened, fascinated.

Fatima's favorite celebrity was Ronald Reagan. "Before he was President of the United States," she would say, "he and Nancy would come over for drinks and dinner. He was always the kindest, sweetest, most polite man. He would help me carry the dirty dishes into the kitchen, and he would insist on helping me clean up after a party."

"Oh, really," responded Queenie. "And how did you like Nancy Reagan?"

"Oh, HER," replied Fatima. "Nancy really wasn't much help."

One day, during a commercial break from their television watching, Queenie let her curiosity get the better of her. "Tell me, Fatima," she asked, "Is it true that Liberace died of AIDS?"

Fatima puffed up in her large shapeless dress. Watching her closely, Queenie would almost swear that helium was expanding her, making her muumuu become even more huge.

"That has never been proved," she sniffed, and she slowly rose from her chair and lumbered out of the room.

"I am so sorry I asked," Queenie tried to call after her.

"Beeyuutiful Dorreetttaaa!" squawked Dr. Dolittle.

After a few weeks of Fatima's stories, Queenie grew weary. "Do you suppose that you could run a few errands for me, Fatima?" she asked. Maybe you would like to get out of the house." But unfortunately, Fatima had never learned to drive an automobile, a fact that had made no difference to Queenie in the beginning but was bothering her more and more now.

Queenie worried that her eyesight was worsening. Sometimes Fatima's blurry muumuu rolled towards her in an engulfing swirl, a brightly colored tidal wave ebbing and flowing. "She's got some Mother Earth qualities," she explained to Moby Dick and Griselda.

When Fatima was particularly overwhelming, Mrs. Adams would sometimes pretend to be sleeping, but she could feel Fatima standing over her, watching and breathing.

Finally, she had to admit that Fatima could never help with the Last Big Project.

"Lord, please take Fatima off my hands," she prayed one night while Fatima was downstairs in the kitchen raking uneaten food off the dishes into the garbage can.

That very night, Queenie awoke suddenly. She did not know why. Griselda and Moby Dick both slept soundly, and Dr. Dolittle was quiet, covered in his cage. As usual, the night light in the hall was burning. The house was quiet. Directly across the hall Queenie could see Fatima's door; she was amazed that she could see it so well and wondered if perhaps she were dreaming.

Suddenly a pajama-clad figure moved along the hallway and stopped at Fatima's door. Old Rex Adams moved—in slow motion—opening the door, then shuffling inside the room. He did not close the door completely. Watching him, Queenie felt her heart grow heavy. Tears smarted in her eyes. "Damned old rusty thing," she said to herself.

He did not stay in the room very long. Suddenly there was a flurry from the other side of the door. Queenie could not understand the words, but she recognized Fatima's voice, pitched high in alarm. The door opened wider, the sound increased in volume, and Rex Adams shuffled out, turned, and headed back down the hall.

Queenie was unable to sleep for the rest of the night, but finally dozed off at dawn.

When she awoke, Fatima was gone. Old Rex called Luke, who, along with his wife Sarah, brought donuts and coffee. Together, Luke and Sarah struggled over the Adams' medications, and together they whispered in the kitchen about what to do next.

"Left in the lurch," Sarah repeated to Queenie again and again. "She just left us in the lurch."

"Kiss me, Queenie!" screeched the parrot.

Old Rex Adams dressed for the day, climbed into his ancient black Cadillac, and inched down the street, heading in the direction of the coffee shop.

The next person that Luke hired to care for his mother was a tiny, neat woman who wore bright white cotton blouses, trim polyester knit slacks and SAS shoes. She was almost the same age as Queenie, but smaller, with crinkled, sallow skin, silver-white hair in short tight curls, and hands swollen with arthritic joints. Her name was Emma Johns, and Queenie thought that she was a very pleasant person.

Emma was spry and moved quickly about, accomplishing every task that Queenie assigned in a fraction of the time the same task had taken Fatima. Emma was quiet, not prone to gossip, and she was clean. She was an excellent cook. "I only hope that I can keep her," Queenie told Luke. "Tell your father that I expect to keep Emma Johns. He will know what I mean."

A week after Mrs. Johns' arrival, she began to slow down, and her breathing became somewhat labored. "Perhaps you need to rest a bit," suggested Queenie. "I do not want you to become ill." She thought of poor Berta Louise, and she shuddered.

As time moved forward, Emma Johns moved more and more slowly, accomplishing less and less. She began to make housekeeping mistakes—using the wrong products, buying the wrong brands, washing colors with whites, adding a bit too much salt.

One afternoon she crept up the wide winding stairs, down the hall, and into Queenie's bedroom. "I must call my daughter long distance in Amarillo," she said. "I really cannot breathe."

"Merciful heavens!" exclaimed Queenie. What to do? What to do? Together, Queenie and Emma Johns managed to dial the daughter's number. "Never mind about reversing the charges," ordered Queenie. "We don't know how to do that anyway, and you can pay me later."

"Beeyoutiful Doretta. Kiss me Quiccckkkk!" squawked Dr. Dolittle.

Having completed the telephone call, the ladies calculated how long it would take for Mrs. Johns' daughter, Katrina, to arrive. "Let's see, she's ninety miles away. That's at least an hour and a half!"

Emma Johns gasped for air. She drew deep audible pulls down into her lungs, frantic with the need to breathe. "I neglected to mention," she said, "that sometimes I get asthma."

"Ohh, Mama! Maaaammmmaaaaaa!"

Queenie Adams told Emma Johns to get up on her bed. She pulled off her oxygen tubing and carefully fitted it around Emma's head. She placed the nosepieces at Emma's nostrils and arranged pillows at her back to help her stay in a semi-upright position.

Queenie spoke deliberately deliberately, "Katrina will arrive in just a little while. Stay calm. Remember that I am here with you." She wracked her brain. Frantic, she looked at Griselda and Moby Dick, whose naps had been disturbed. "What more should I do?" she asked.

As Queenie and Emma Johns lay together on her bed, it occurred to Queenie that she should pray. She folded her hands and whispered. "Lord, please take Mrs. Johns off my hands, but please don't let her die until she gets back to Amarillo."

"Mmmmaaammmaaaa!"

Mrs. Emma Johns left on a stretcher in an ambulance.

Queenie Adams remarked to everybody—her husband, her doctor, her son, her daughter-in-law—that that was more excitement than she had experienced in quite some time.

"Are you all right, Mother?" Luke asked, as he helped Sarah rearrange the sheets and plump the pillows behind Queenie's head.

"I just need some rest," she assured them. "Let me take a little nap." She closed her eyes, and they tiptoed away. She lay in her darkened room, thinking about the past few days, and wondered if her prayers about Fatima and Emma Johns had truly been answered by God. "The Lord works in mysterious ways," she concluded.

Then she decided to call Berta Louise one last time and give her another opportunity to help with the Project. Dialing in the dark, Queenie made a telephone call to Berta Louise.

"Please come," she begged. "Come help me with my Final Project, and you will never have to come again. I swear it on a stack of Bibles. By the way, I think that you should know that I'm in pretty good with God."

Two days after Emma John's departure, Berta Louise came back to Queenie Adams. Berta Louise returned, wearing her starched white uniform, her white nurses' shoes, and her royal blue turban. When Berta Louise smiled, her right front tooth matched the golden hoops that hung from her earlobes. As efficient as ever, she sat Queenie up in a wheelchair, adjusted the oxygen tank, and rolled the chair and the tank down the hall from Queenie's bedroom, which Queenie had not left for months. Berta Louise had her middle-aged sons, Glenrose and Johnny, come to carry Queenie—along with oxygen and wheelchair—down the wide, winding staircase to the ground floor.

"Now, Missy," she stated, "If I'm going to work myself to death for you on this project, you going to cooperate with me. And I won't put up with no sniveling or complaining."

First, they outlined their project, writing their goals on a calendar that they posted in the breakfast room. "We mark off every day from now on," Berta Louise announced. "I expect to be finished with this here job before Christmastime."

They started in the basement. Sitting in the wheelchair, Queenie directed Berta Louise, who began to make piles of family belongings: "Throw away," "Give away," and "Keep." Without hesitation, Queenie would gasp out, "Throw it away!" "Give it away!" or "Keep it!"

Berta Louise put the objects that had been placed in the first two piles into garbage bags and then she carefully labeled them. The objects in the "Keep" pile she rearranged neatly on shelves. The two women went through old papers, old letters, camping and fishing equipment, hunting clothes, bats, balls and gloves, tennis rackets, dishes, pots and pans, kerosene lamps, pictures, fruit jars, luggage, discarded furniture, little red wagons, a baby carriage, army cots, tricycles, a bike, a unicycle and a birdcage. For throw-aways and give-aways, Berta Louise neatly labeled each individual item that would not fit into a plastic sack, and carefully placed it in a specific area in the basement. At the end of each day her sons would come, driving their ancient maroon pick-up, and take the sacks to the town dump or the Salvation Army.

Occasionally during the workday, the women heard Dr. Dolittle upstairs screeching, "Dorreettta! Kisss Mee!" "Sometimes he would call out, "Maammmaa! Oh, Maaammmmmaaaa!"

"Something the matter with your old bird," said Berta Louise.

"I think that he's just a little confused," answered Queenie.

It took Queenie and Berta Louise two weeks to get through with the basement. "No naps for you, Missy," stated Berta Louise. "No television either, no books-on-tape, no conversations with your old friends. We on a roll, and I expects us to keep the roll going."

"Fine with me," answered Queenie. "Whatever you say."

Next, they tackled the main floor of the mansion. "This is going to be a nightmare," lamented Queenie."

"Buckle up and look smart, Missy," stated Berta Louise. "We going to do this, and we going to do it in record time."

"On this floor, the` throw away' pile and the `give away' pile will be small. But I want you to label all of the items that we keep with the relatives' names–so that they can be given to the proper persons later."

"Later than what?" asked Berta Louise.

"You know, just later." instructed Queenie.

"Oh, you mean LATER, after you go to Glory," surmised Berta Louise.

So item by item, treasure by treasure, collection by collection, art object by art object, picture by picture, vase by vase, book by book, cushion by cushion, tablecloth by tablecloth, napkin by napkin, dish by dish, tray by tray, Berta Louise labeled with sticky labels supplied by Luke's secretary, as Queenie instructed her, one by one. The Oriental rugs, the Tiffany lamps, the large mirrors, the jardinières, the candelabra, the sculptures, and the furniture were listed on separate sheets of paper, for Luke to keep at the bank.

It took six weeks for Berta Louise and Queenie to sort through all the items on the main floor.

"You know, I think that this is fun," announced Queenie one day. "I almost wish that this project would never end."

"Well, I guess not!" exclaimed Berta Louise. "But you ain't doing most of the work!"

Some days Queenie wanted to discuss deep theological matters, but she found that Berta Louise was not interested.

"What about you, Berta Louise?" she once asked. "Do you ever wonder about how things will be after we're gone? About how things will be when we reach heaven? Do you think that you and I will know each other there?"

"Nope. I don't wonder about it one bit."

"My life is just about over, Berta Louise. Do you think that God will take me soon?"

Berta Louise sighed, "Any time now suit me just fine."

"Ha ha. You are so funny you make me tired. Tell me, Berta Louise. When I die, do you think that very many people will come to my funeral?"

"Law, yes, Missy. Everybody come. Everybody celebrate."

They were silent for a while. Then Queenie said, "You know, I feel like the song, "Old Man River." I'm tired of living and scared of dying."

"Ain't no reason to be scared. Why, you be the prettiest old angel up there. Best dressed, too. You look so smart the Lord God Almighty invite you to sit beside Him at the dinner table!"

This was the gist of their conversations, as room by room they examined every article, every belonging, and every object that the Adams owned. Early every morning, Glenrose and Johnny came to carry Queenie in her wheelchair down the stairs from her bedroom. Often Griselda rode on Queenie's lap. Always Moby Dick followed, usually nipping and yapping. And always Dr. Dolittle squawked, until he too had been brought down in his cage to join the others. At the end of the day, Johnny and Glenrose would reappear, silently carrying Queenie back up the stairs, while Berta Louise rounded up the dog, the cat, and the parrot.

"Why are Glenrose and Johnny so quiet? Why won't

they even talk to me?" asked Queenie one day.

"They thinks you working their mama too hard," answered Berta Louise.

"Why ARE you doing this, Mother?" asked Luke more than once. "You are positively wearing yourself out."

"I have things on my agenda," she always answered.

They spent only two weeks sorting through items on the second floor. The guest bedrooms were already relatively well organized, but Queenie's room took almost a week, which was filled with worry, hesitation and discussion.

"I'm sorry to be so sentimental," Queenie said, "but all of these mementos remind me of happy days in the past. If I didn't have such a big house, this would not be such a problem."

"Well, Missy, we all has our crosses to bear," answered Berta Louise. "You has this great big old mansion, and I has you."

"Very funny, Berta Louise. Very funny, ha ha," answered Queenie.

"We is just two little old ladies who is real tired," stated Berta Louise, as she folded and patted down a nightgown in Queenie's lingerie drawer.

"While we are giving things away, I want to tell you this," Queenie gasped. "I'm planning to donate my organs to science. I need to tell Luke to bring papers for me to sign."

"Naw! Who want your old organs? Ain't one part of you ain't done wore out! No part of me, neither."

Queenie sat in silence and concentrated on breathing, as Berta Louise worked. Finally, Queenie added, "I think I'll tell my husband to donate his old organ to the First Methodist Church."

The two ladies rocked with merriment.

Only one room on the second floor had been left intact. They had left old Rex Adams' room down the hall completely alone. "That's his business, not mine," Queenie told Berta Louise.

"Law, I remember when my first husband passed on," Berta Louise said suddenly. "He Glenrose's daddy, and he passed over thirty years ago. Him suddenly going that way a big shock to me. I's not ready for that."

"I remember that too, Berta Louise."

"Remember what he look like all laid out in his coffin? All dressed up in that black suit and bow tie? With his moustache sticking out?"

"I really don't remember it, Berta Louise."

"He look like a damn cat."

The ballroom on the third floor had served as Queenie's costume shop. It was filled with props and costumes of all sizes and descriptions. After Glenrose and Johnny had carried Queenie, the cat, the dog, and the bird to the third floor, Queenie said, "Now I know that you dread the way you think I'll behave up here. Emotional and all. I promise I won't cry. No tears, no regrets, no silly memories."

"Now, Queenie, you be as silly as you want. I remember just about everybody in town dressed up in these outfits at one time or other." Berta Louise held up a black and white striped clown suit and red wig." Law, law, these costumes mighty fine."

"Let's save three of the best costumes for each of the grandchildren and great-grandchildren—mine and yours—then we'll give the rest away. That will be our plan of action."

The costumes hung on custom-made clothing rods. Hats and shoes were categorized in boxes, and standing scattered in the attic were three mannequins- sporting a Cleopatra outfit, a Marie Antoinette dress and wig, and a Davy Crockett buckskin frontiersman suit. Arranged against one wall were ironing boards, sewing supplies and two sewing machines.

Lickety-split, Berta Louise sorted through the costumes as Queenie directed, determining what to save for their grandchildren and what to give away.

In a richly embossed metallic gold antique trunk, they found Queenie's wedding dress. "Oh, yes, we shall save this," she said. "Oh, yes, indeed."

Queenie had Luke call the chair of the drama department at the local high school, as well as the ministers at the churches, and the Worthy Matron of the Eastern Star. He gave these people the rest of the costumes. Before Queenie and Berta Louise knew it, all the costumes were gone.

Then Queenie asked Berta Louise to retrieve the lace wedding dress, and to bring the sharpest scissors from her sewing basket. "Now cut," she instructed, "and keep on cutting until I tell you to stop."

"Cuuut!" screamed Dr. Dolittle.

Throughout the afternoon Berta Louise would hold up pieces of lace for Queenie's approval. "Not small enough," she would say. "I want you to keep on cutting until the pieces are about the size of butterfly wings."

When the cutting was completed, the two old ladies opened the ballroom window and flung out the tiny scraps of lace, which softly floated against an orange West Texas sky. Weightless and transparent, they swirled out, easy on the autumn wind.

When Berta Louise pronounced the Final Project finished, Queenie asked her to figure up what was owed her. Queenie closely examined the paper upon which Berta Louise had scribbled her figures. "Now double that," Queenie instructed. "Please take a check out of my purse. Fill it out and I shall sign it." Her breathing was labored. "I want you to stay one more night. I want you to do just one last thing. Let's get this business over. I have the pills we need."

"No, I ain't staying. I's going home."

Queenie caught her old friend's hand. "I am very grateful for all you've done, Berta Louise." She paused. "All right, then, come back tomorrow. Leave your check on the nightstand in my bedroom. I'll sign it later. And don't worry. No one will notice if I just keel over. No one will care."

Berta Louise pulled her hand away and put her dark face up close to Queenie's. "Listen, Queenie, you be surprised. Us likes to know you here—up in this big old house—you our dear old Queenie."

"You will do this one last thing. Then our Final Project will be complete. I expect you to be here tomorrow." Queenie's voice was barely audible.

"I'll come but I ain't going to do what you ask. For over fifty years I does what you say but not tomorrow. I ain't got no room for what you got in mind."

Glenrose and Johnny appeared at the ballroom door and carried Queenie back to her bedroom. They looked at neither Queenie nor their mother. Berta Louise tucked Queenie into bed, adjusted her oxygen tubes, and poured her a glass of cold water. After telling Queenie goodbye, Berta Louise slowly crept down the stairway and out the door to Glenrose's waiting pickup.

The next morning, Queenie Adams lay against the pillows, breathing the oxygen deeply. She opened her eyes and looked around her room. Such a pretty room with such lovely things! Collected over a lifetime, artistically arranged, worth a fortune! The linens on her bed—cool and clean— had been pulled tightly. Quite comfortable. The perfect way to end a life. She folded her hands over her chest and dozed, waiting for Berta Louise.

She was aware of a shuffling noise inside the room. Opening her eyes, she saw old Rex leading Glenrose in. The men stood together beside her bed.

Suddenly, Griselda stood up, arched her back and hissed, then jumped off the edge of the bed and tunneled under the bed skirt. Her ragged tail stuck out from under the bed ruffle in its entirety and twitched nervously. At the same time, Moby Dick opened his filmy eyes, blinked, yawned, and cuddled more closely to Queenie. Dr. Dolittle opened his eyes as wide as possible and squawked, "Oooohhhh, Queenie!"

"My Mama took sick last night," Glenrose began. "Doctor at the Emergency say she have a stroke. She passed early this morning." He waited while Queenie stared at him in disbelief. "Yesterday my Mama say to me if she took sick," he hesitated, cleared his throat, and continued, "if she die, I has to come at once and tell you something, Miss Queenie. Made me promise to come and say it."

Queenie sat up in the center of her bed. Her silver hair stood straight up, and her round gray eyes pierced through the morning air. She peered at Glenrose, who held his hat in his hands.

"Well, what is it, Glenrose? Tell me what she said." Queenie thought her own voice sounded very far away.

Glenrose spoke slowly. "She say to tell you she be waiting. That's all she say. Don't be afraid. She waiting."

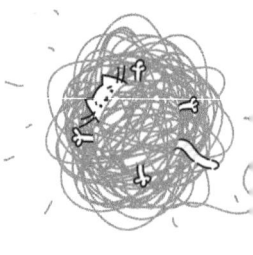

RETRIBUTION

Mary Kay Demsey was famous for her Christmas letters. Although *famous* might be too strong an adjective, she was, nevertheless, remarkably popular with those friends and relatives who received her annual holiday missive.

There was always something to write about.

She only briefly mentioned her family members. Didn't go on and on about her children's or grandchildren's achievements nor her husband's accomplishments. Never wrote about health, rarely referred to death, didn't elaborate on family trips or exotic vacations. If she ever took on these subjects, which are familiar in many Christmas letters, it was in a light-hearted, satiric way. Frequently she used that same casual tone to deal with current events.

In 2017, which may go down in American history as "The Year of National Groping," she focused on that very subject. As she was deliciously composing her message, she felt almost virginal, and grateful that she'd never been subjected to a grope by any rude, horny guy.

"Thank God for my sweet husband," she said to herself.

In her nightly prayers Mary Kay said, 'Thank you, Lord, that I have never been sexually harassed or groped. As the Baptists say, *Thank you, Jesus!*'

Here in part is Mary Kay's 2017 Christmas letter:

Dear Friends and Family,

You all know a lot about me—where and how I grew up. And most of you know that I've visited many places and met lots of people. A meaningful life of great experiences. But I feel left out of the mainstream, because recently something has come to my attention. My life has suffered a bitter omission. At 75 years of age, I must confess – I have never been groped.

Never groped – not by a teacher, preacher, politician, businessman, doctor, entertainer, slobbering senile old uncle, not even a dog-catcher.

I'm beginning to wonder if I've even been groped by my husband. He says No, he's never groped anyone. Apparently, we are the only gropeless people in America.

From there on, the letter referred to family members and friends in a light-hearted way with few or no details.

Two days after sending the letter, Mary Kay began receiving calls, emails, and notes from people who said they loved her letter about groping. She was relieved that she had offended no one.

A week later, Mary Kay and her husband met with friends for dinner. These were three male golfing buddies and their wives. Their routine was to meet in someone's home for cocktails and then to go out to dinner together. It was a congenial group: the men had the love of golf in common; the wives had in common putting up with their golf-crazed husbands.

Each couple had received Mary Kay's Christmas letter, but no one mentioned it. After a round of drinks, the men emerged from their TV lair, where they had been watching sports, and they announced that it was time to drive to the restaurant.

As her husband led her to their car, each of the remaining three men approached her from behind. Two of them pinched her buttocks, and one popped the back of her bra. Then the silly old farts turned to her and laughed, "Now you can't say you've never been groped!" They heehawed like donkeys.

Mary Kay's husband acted oblivious to the event, totally unaware.

But Mary Kay stood as still as a statue, while she asked herself, *what can I say without making a scene? And ruining everyone's evening? And infuriating my husband?* She had no answer, so she gritted her teeth, put on a half-hearted smile, and began walking again.

The couples went on to dinner; the men laughing and talking, the women strangely silent.

Later, while getting ready for bed, Mary Kay told her husband, "I think your friends misinterpreted my letter about groping. I wasn't complaining; I was bragging about the caliber of men I've always known. So, I didn't appreciate their ganging up on me and pinching my ass. My God, they're eighty years old! They should know better. They *do* know better!"

"Oh, you asked for it in that letter," he answered. "What's the matter with you? Can't you take a joke? Honey, it's no big deal. Get over it."

"Listen, buster! I'm not going to put up with that again! The next time one of those old coots touches my rear, I'm gonna scream bloody whorehouse murder!"

"You'll do no such thing. You'll put up with it. Women always do."

Mary Kay couldn't accept the fact that she was a seventy-five-year-old gropee. She planned a luncheon – complete with crystal, china, and sterling silver. She spread out her best linens and ordered an elaborate centerpiece from the florist. She had the meal prepared and served by the city's finest caterer, who wore a white jacket and gloves.

Her three guests were the wives of the gropers.

After the waiter served bananas foster for dessert, Mary Kay asked her friends to join her in the living room, out of earshot.

They settled into comfortable chairs, and Mary Kay brought up the subject of groping. Gradually the topic became personal, and she described their husbands' behavior.

"They thought it was funny, but the entire incident hurt my feelings," she added.

"They'd had too much to drink," said one wife.

"That's no excuse," said another.

"I don't blame you for being offended. They owe you an apology," said the third.

What they didn't say but they all wondered was, has *my husband been groping women all along?*

"The worst part was the way my husband reacted," Mary Kay said. "I'm going to make him regret it."

"What will you do?" someone asked.

"I don't know for sure, but something subtle, like gluing strips of sandpaper inside his jockey shorts."

Everybody laughed.

"What about washing his underpants and hanging them on a cactus to dry?" from another.

"Break the zippers in all of his trousers, even his golfing pants. Make *him* take them to the tailor's to be replaced."

"Sprinkle red hot pepper in his underwear. When there's the least bit of moisture, he'll go crazy."

"Cut out the front of every pair of his drawers. That'll leave his tallywacker exposed to the zipper in his pants. He'll be rubbed raw."

The ladies laughed until they cackled. Finally, someone looked at her watch and announced it was time to go pick up her grandchildren from school. The others stood to leave as well.

As each of Mary Kay's friends said goodbye, she hugged her hostess with tears in her eyes and said, "I'm sorry my husband was rude to you."

Mary Kay followed up on her plan to make her old

husband suffer. She tried a different tactic every day for a week. She knew that he would consider it a masculine weakness to complain of itching or soreness in his nether region.

The next time all the couples got together for dinner, Mary Kay noticed that all four of the men walked funny.

At the end of their meal, one of the ladies stood and asked the other women to stand also. Then they all laughed and high-fived.

"Well, we did it," the first one said.

"Yep, and we can do it again, if necessary," said another.

"You boys better watch it now," said the third. "We're on to you."

The old men sat at the table with their heads down, making no eye contact.

"You guys owe me an apology," Mary Kay said.

"You owe us all an apology," said another woman.

"We're not going to put up with your sexist silliness any longer," chimed a third.

Then the fourth lady ordered, "So get up off your sore old butts and apologize."

The men slowly rose. Looking down, they mumbled, "I'm sorry." Then they quickly sat down.

"Not good enough!" Mary Kay announced. "Each of you spoke with no feeling whatsoever. Girls, I don't accept their puny apologies. The only way I can reconcile my humiliation is to take a lovely, long trip. Maybe a cruise. With friends." She pulled several travel brochures from her purse and passed them to the other women, who looked through them greedily. She nodded at the men. "This is going to cost you, bigtime."

"Are you expecting us to take you?" asked one of them.

"Good grief, no!" answered Mary Kay. "We're particular. We don't travel with gropers."

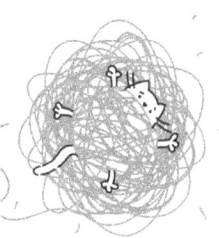

LOVE, SQUALOR, AND THE MEXICAN MEN

It was the last day of classes before Spring Break of my freshman year at the University of Arkansas, home of the Razorbacks. *Soooouuuuiiieee Pig!* I drove home to spend a week with my parents. It was not my choice. I was, like, at great odds with them because they were, like, driving me crazy.

My English professor, Dr. Higgins, said I used the word *like* too much. He sorta reminded me of my dad. He was picky and constantly complained about the way we wrote. He was what you would call a very critical guy. Anyway, this "like" thing is what he called "Valley Girl Talk" which first invaded the sorority houses in California and then spread like wildfire through the rest of the nation. He wanted to stamp it out. Just to please him and to try to pass his course, I was working on eliminating "like" from my vocabulary, except when I said, "I really like somebody."

Dr. Higgins was too hard on us. I flunked, or nearly flunked, every one of his assignments. It wasn't my fault.

He was too picky. When I asked him if I could do anything to bring my grade up, he gave me a list of books by this J. D. Salinger guy to check out of the library and read over spring break. Then when I got back to school some other students and I would meet with him for a discussion of our reading. He said he wanted to be sure we actually did the reading, and not copy synopses off the internet. In other words, he thought we might cheat.

Dr. H. had no sympathy for the fact that I had to spend the entire week with my parents in our little podunky Arkansas town of Rennieville — population of 6,000. Before Spring Break, I was invited to two exciting places. One, a group of my friends was headed for Beaver Creek to spend the week on the slopes. The other invitation was to Padre Island, which everybody says is one of the most fun places in the universe.

I probably would have chosen Padre, especially since I wanted to work on my tan, and the guys there are hot, but my dad, the control freak, said, "No, Angela, absolutely not! Any daughter of mine who can't manage to pass her courses during the first semester of her freshman year will not be taking fine expensive vacations." So, he made me come home right after my classes. I was, like, furious!

My dad was the only ophthalmologist in our small burg, and he had a high opinion of himself. Sometimes in private I called him "Mr. Wonderful," just to be sarcastic. Anyway, I knew he'd be full of lectures and general gripeyness all week and I dreaded it and would rather drink scalding poison than put up with those two self-righteous fuddieduddiess, my mom and my dad.

What's more, the old man had a plan. Since I'd be home anyway, with nothing to do during the day — his words, not mine — I had to work at his office, and give Marie, one of his office girls, a break. That way Marie could spend the week home with her kids, and I could earn a little money. Big deal! It was supposed to be my vacation! *Had he lost his mind?*

When I appealed to Mom, she looked at me in that sweet simpering witless way of hers and said, "Angie, I think you should mind your daddy." So I was, like, furious at her, also.

What a couple of old farts.

I was the youngest of three children. My brother, who was twenty-four, was in law school at Vanderbilt University. He got his B.A. in political science at Vanderbilt, also. Probably the smartest one in the family. My sister, two years younger than he, was a senior at the University of Illinois. A pre-med major, she planned to be an ophthalmologist like Dad. Both Bro and Sis stayed on their campuses to work on special projects. My mother was a Stay-At-Home, but she had taught English while my dad was in med school, many eons ago.

I was proud to say that I came from a highly educated family. But the truth was, they really got on my nerves. All I wanted to accomplish during that week was the special project of getting a tan!

During my first weekend home, not one interesting

thing happened. One night Dad asked Mom and me if we would like to "Take in a movie"—that's how he put it! Of course, I said no. I'd rather die than be seen at a movie with those two old crows. They went without me, and I spent the evening with our dog, Spooky, and our cat, Ophelia, who had a new litter of kittens.

While my folks were gone, I wished I had a boyfriend, a drink, and a cigarette. In that order.

My dad meant what he said about making me work, and I rode with him to his office early Monday morning. I had several chores — all of which were complicated. Too confusing. Dad snapped at me a couple of times, which made it worse. It was a day from, like, hell.

The only neat thing about working there was I got to wear a cute, colorful jacket every day. Marie let me wear hers, and I started the week with a blue one. I looked professional, but couldn't do a damn thing, like, right!

Tuesday was, like, a little better but not much. I wore a yellow jacket and tried to be bright and cheerful. At one point I led Mrs. Riley into the examining room but attached Mr. Butler's chart to the door. This made my dad furious, but he said nothing, only glared at me. After the mix-up was corrected and Mrs. Riley was gone, Dad sort of exploded.

Reminded me of the time Dr. Higgins got so mad at my roommate Jennifer we thought he might have a heart attack. It happened in class, just a few days after the second semester started. We were studying short stories and he was trying to teach us how to analyze fiction. We had been assigned to read J. D. Salinger's "For Esme— with Love and Squalor."

Dr. Higgins wanted us to discuss the story, and he called upon Jennifer. "And what kind of story is this, Jennifer?" he asked.

"I don't know, sir," she answered, "because I don't know what 'squalor' is."

"Don't know what SQUALOR is! Good God, girl, do you not own a dictionary? What in heaven's name would keep you from looking the word up? Don't know what SQUALOR is! I suppose you don't. Living in your overprotected safe little world."

We thought Dr. Higgins was so dramatic he should, like, be on television. After his hysterical fit, he gave us an impromptu assignment. Every one of us had to write a definition of "squalor" as well as give an example of some part of the world where people live in squalor.

"Keep it short," he said. "One paragraph will do. You may use my dictionary if you wish, and I will give you about fifteen minutes."

For my in-class assignment I wrote,

"Squalor is the condition of being filthy and miserable or being dirty and wretched in appearance. An excellent example of squalor can be found at the foot of the Ozark Mountains in my hometown of Rennieville. There, almost two thousand people—mostly men from Mexico—live in very poor conditions. Nearly all of them are employed at the local Byron chicken plant. They work ten to twelve-hour shifts, with few breaks, at minimum wages. The plant is open 24 hours a day. When the men are not working, they walk around the town or if the weather is good, they sit outside their homes—on stoops or porches. They try to stay outside as much as possible, because they live in sub-standard rental apartments, rat-infested homes, or trailer houses. They sleep an average of eight men to a room, and they usually pay about $100 a month each for their rent. They are homesick and they are poor and maybe even hopeless, but they continue to work. Every Saturday morning you can see these men, lined up at the post office, sending most of the money they have earned back home to their families, who live in even worse squalor."

When he handed my paper back to me at the next class meeting, Dr. Higgins said, "I believe that you have some promise, Angela."

On Wednesday I wore a hot pink jacket to the office. It was a pretty good day in that Dad did not yell or glower at me. He even took me to lunch. I decided he might be trying harder to get along.

That night, though, he invited me to go with him to the City Council meeting, along with a group of Rennieville citizens who want something to be done about the living conditions of the Mexican men. The City Council had formed a committee, like, several months ago, and had asked my dad to serve as chairman. He researched other towns with chicken plants and lots of Hispanic workers to find out how they've solved their housing problems.

"The trouble is," Dad stated at the dinner table, "many

of the townspeople own run-down property that they want to rent to these guys—with very little maintenance and almost no thoughts of safety or sanitation. Some of those houses don't have plumbing; some have unsafe electrical wiring. Some are over-run by rodents. And our city officials have been looking the other way while the slumlords get rich. Couple these poor living conditions with the fact that this whole state is crawling with immigration agents, and the Mexicans are as nervous as hell. It's a mess. We've got a disaster just waiting to happen."

I knew that Dad was right, but I couldn't stand to hear him preaching again. So, I refused to go to the meeting with him. I watched him gather his notes, along with his committee's proposals. Then he left the house, alone.

I thought about, like, suddenly changing my mind. Instead, I watched TV for a while and played with Ophelia's babies. When she got cross with me and started carrying her kittens away, I grabbed that Ryecatcher book that I had brought from the university library, and I started, like, reading.

On Thursday I decided that working for Dad was too damn tiring. You must stand on your feet all day, running up and down the halls on these hard floors. It's a killer. And it's stressful. He is such a perfectionist! Some contact lens came in from the manufacturer, and something about the order wasn't right, and I thought Dad would go ballistic!

That day at noon, instead of going out to lunch, I went with Mom to help her deliver Meals on Wheels to a bunch of shitty old people. Her good friend Mary Helen usually went with her, but Mary Helen was in Texas helping her daughter with her new baby.

Anyway, the routine was that Mom would drive the route and I would take the trays of food to the door. The old people are, like, REALLY OLD and are so happy to see you they nearly talk your arms and legs off. Some are pretty sick, too. You have to deliver the right stuff and also take the order for their meal for the following day, so you sorta have to concentrate.

One thing that happened at one of the houses was not exactly fun. Mrs. O'Conner, a shriveled-up, fuzzy-haired lady in a purple print dress answered the door, and she was crying.

I called Mom to get out of the car and come quick. There was not really an emergency, but Mrs. O'Conner was upset because her neighbors—a young Mexican couple—had been hauled away in the middle of the night. The young woman—Anita was her name—had run over to Mrs. O'Conner and begged her to take care of their cat. Mrs. O'Conner had agreed to do it, and had the cat there in her house, but she was afraid for Anita.

Mom asked, "Who took Anita and her husband away? Could you see anything?"

Mrs. O'Conner sobbed and sobbed. "I couldn't see anything. I couldn't see anyone. I don't know what happened to them! But I'm afraid they've been deported!"

Mom tried her best to comfort Mrs. O'Conner. After we finished our route, she reported her concerns to the Meals on Wheels headquarters. By the time I made it back to Dad's office, I had caused the other girls to miss their full lunch hour and I was, like, shaking.

I was so unhappy I thought if I could put up with Mom and Dad for only three more days, I'd have it made. I knew one thing: I was going to do better about my grades. I simply must not get kicked out of school! Dad said something about me taking Marie's place permanently and let me tell you — if I thought I would have to stay in Rennieville and work for him permanently or even for the summer, I would cut my throat.

My goal was to pull my grades up—I knew I could do it, just had to concentrate and get organized! Had to stop cutting classes! Had to start doing the assignments! When I passed my classes, I would insist that I be allowed to go to summer school to make up the courses I failed first semester. Maybe I could get a part-time job—maybe Dr. Higgins or one of his buddies in the English Department could use someone like me. After all, now I had office experience!

Part of my resolution was a result of the sad Meals on Wheels incident and part was a result of something I sorta accidentally found out. When bills came in at the office, it was my job to slit them open for Dad. I sorta opened his bank statement by mistake and found out something. He, like, wasn't nearly as rich as I'd thought. This revelation had me worried, big-time.

This was the day I wore the mauve jacket. I consider mauve a funeral color.

Friday was St. Patrick's Day, and we all wore green at

the office. Sonya, Dad's office manager, brought chocolate cupcakes with green icing and green punch. She gave everybody a cute St. Pat's card, and that was the extent of our celebration.

What a crappy job.

Dad got very mad at me. Mrs. Morgan, about a hundred and fifty years old, had gone to visit her daughter in California, and she'd lost her glasses. The daughter called the office in a panic earlier this week, and Dad ordered new glasses right away. They came, Dad checked them, and I was supposed to mail them ASAP. Well, I forgot. When Dad found out, he exploded. So, I was in big trouble with The Control Freak. Couldn't he lighten up just a little? God, he got on my nerves!

He said that the next day, Saturday morning, I had to, like, get up early and run down to the post office to mail those stupid glasses. So much for sleeping 'til noon on Saturday!

I asked Mom if she would run the errand for me, but she said, "Angela, when will you ever learn?"

Ever learn what?

I tried to figure out what was the matter with my dad. Why he was so morbid. I'd heard him talk about the Civil Rights Movement and the war in Vietnam. He said that he was too young to go with his cousins to Mississippi to march with the black people, and he was also too young to go off to Washington to protest the war. But he said that both of those national problems had an impact on his life. I don't see how, and I don't see why. But I finally decided that Mom and Dad were sorry they didn't get to be hippies.

Humorless grumpbutts.

Reading these Salinger stories every night made me think more about Mom and Dad and what they've done with their lives and also about what I'm going to do with mine. In "For Esme—With Love and Squalor," Esme wants a story written for her exclusively, a story full of meaning. In "Franny and Zooey," Franny wants to find God. In *The Catcher in the Rye*, Phoebe wants her brother to be safe and happy. And in my story, I didn't know what I wanted. But I did have a tremendous yearning.

Saturday started off all wrong and left me quivering.

In the first place, I overslept, having stayed up late to finish the book of nine Salinger stories. Dad knocked on my door at 8:00 a.m. and told me to get down to the post office immediately, so that I could get in line with my package—Mrs. Morgan's glasses.

Yesterday I had, like, begged him not to make me stand in line at the post office with all those Mexican men, who worked at the chicken plant and sent weekly money orders home to their families. I begged him again not to make me do it.

"Get some clothes on," he said. "Maybe you'll get there before all those guys arrive. You know that you're responsible for this situation. You are the one who forgot to mail the package, and you are the one who slept late."

Since the weather had been so warm, I threw on some shorts and a tee-shirt and pulled my hair up in a pony-tail. I threw a cap on my head and grabbed some sunglasses.

Didn't even brush my teeth.

When I arrived at the post office, there were at least fifty men in line outside, maybe close to a hundred. So, holding my package, I took my place at the end of the line. I was furious with Mom and Dad. After all, I had missed a week of fun—only to be humiliated on the town square, standing in line with a bunch of strange foreign men! But most of all, I was pissed that my dad got to control my life in this shitty one-horse town in the awful state of Arkansas where nobody would ever want to spend even one moment of their time if they had any sense!

Since I was, like, wearing shorts, I would have assumed that the Mexican men would have stared at me. I would have thought that they would be loud and rude and that they might make all sorts of vulgar comments. But they totally ignored me, and I even thought at one point, *"Am I invisible?"*

Pretty soon there were lots of men behind me, and we stood outside on the sidewalk, with the line winding up the post office steps. It was a beautiful day, and redbud trees and dogwoods bloomed up and down the streets along the town square. Bright yellow daffodils and red tulips filled the flowerbeds at the courthouse, across the street from the post office. I began to relax and enjoy the scenery as the warm sun beat down on my legs.

The post office door was held open by whatever man happened to be standing in the doorway, but the line moved too slowly. The men were very quiet. Now and then one would call, "*Hola!*" to someone coming out.

Now and then a couple of them would quietly converse.

— Como *esta?*

—*Estoy bien.*

— Que *pasa?*

—*Nada. Estoy esperando en la linea.*

Finally, I reached the front door and got inside the building. I was able to see what had held up the line: there was only one worker there—-Sandy Griffin, our postmistress. At the next two stations were signs saying, "Closed."

The men inside were even more quiet than the ones outside. If they even saw me, they didn't show it. They were nearly all pretty small and fairly dark. They looked clean and some had drippy hair, as if they had come straight from the showers at the plant. They smelled of soap and after-shave and wore colorless clothes. I decided this was a pretty interesting experience, something to tell my friends back at school, something to, like, write an essay about for Dr. Higgins.

Suddenly, an arm reached over my shoulder and grabbed the man just ahead of me. Roughly pulled him out of the line. We all stared as a tall man in uniform yanked him across the marble floor. The small man stumbled over his own feet and fell, hitting his forehead on the corner of the table where I had stood every day this week, putting stamps on my dad's mail. We could hear the thump of his head when it hit. He fell to the floor, and the taller one was on top of him. Suddenly the other men—the ones in line—began to talk. They never shouted, but they all spoke rapidly in Spanish and all I could make out was, "La *inmigra!*"

Only when the tall man stood up did I realize he was an INS cop. He was almost twice the size of the Mexican. He pulled the man's arms behind his back and snapped handcuffs on him... Then the huge cop pulled the Mexican to his feet, and blood streamed from a gash in his forehead. It ran down his white tee-shirt.

Something happened to me. I can't explain it, but I felt as if I were outside my body watching the whole scene. I had no control; I just snapped.

"What are you doing?" I screamed at the officer as I ran into him. I tried to grab his arm. "Don't you realize that you've hurt somebody's FATHER?"

By then another cop had come into the post office. He pushed me, and the Mexican men backed away, while I fell back into line. The two American officers left with the bleeding man stumbling between them.

Dr. Higgins would agree with me that the entire event was surreal.

It kept on being surreal while I moved up to the window to mail Mrs. Morgan's glasses and as I woodenly left the post office, walking down the steps and down the sidewalk. I got into my car and drove straight home. When I turned into our driveway, I saw my dad. He had just come from the nursery with fertilizer and shrubs to plant along the east side of the house. Suddenly he looked old and thin and terribly tired. Only then did I start crying. I thought that I would never stop.

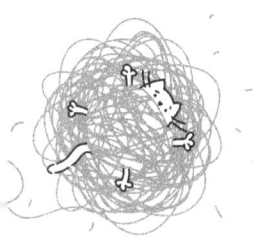

A PERFECT WEDDING FOR EMILY

"Mother and Dad are no trouble at all," my sister Jill says when she calls to ask me to come for a few days early for her daughter Emily's June wedding. "They just need a little help with their medication." Jill wants me to put my law practice on hold and drive from Memphis to West Texas in order to take our folks off her hands. Although our parents still live by themselves in their own home, Jill considers herself their caregiver. She and her husband live three blocks from the folks, and she checks on them frequently every day. She's an old mother hen.

Of course, as Emily's only aunt, I say, "Yes, I'll be happy to help. It's the least I can do."

My father takes offense. He calls me on my cell phone, just as I'm finishing a legal brief.

"We need no help. No supervision. You girls act as if we're about to fall into the grave. Both of us." He pauses to cough. "Well, maybe your mother needs a little attention occasionally, but not me." He has this tirade on the day before I'm supposed to show up as substitute caregiver.

"You may not need me, but I'm coming anyway," I tell him.

I drive west, under a huge expanse of azure sky, from old southern Memphis to the Texas Panhandle, and I finally reach the small town where I grew up. The town that flourished during my youth, when it was on Route 66, now is shrunken and partially dilapidated. I drive down Main Street, then turn onto the elm-lined street where I once lived, and park at the two-story red brick house, which my parents vow they will never leave.

After hugs and kisses, I install myself in the guest room, across the hall from my parents' bedroom. "To keep an eye on you," I joke with Dad. But he isn't amused.

Earlier in the spring, Mother fell and broke her arm. Immediately after my arrival today, she shows me her injury. After rolling up her long-sleeved blue silk blouse, she says, "Here. Does this look right?" Mother's arm has a zigzag shape.

"Of course not!" I answer. "What does Jill say about it?"

"I haven't told her. She's been busy with the wedding. I don't want to be a bother."

"Does your arm hurt?"

"Oh, yes," she answers. "The pain would kill me, if I didn't have medication."

"Mother! Don't be such a martyr!"

"The problem will correct itself," she sniffs.

"I'm taking you to your doctor tomorrow," I tell her.

"Listen," she says, grabbing my sleeve with her good hand. "I'd rather be eaten alive by wild dogs than mess up Emily's wedding! Don't you dare mention this to your sister!"

"O.K. I understand." I move away from her clutch. "We'll wait until after the wedding."

"You bet your sweet life we will, young lady," Mother says.

After unpacking, I put steaks on the grill and potatoes in the oven, throw together a salad, and call Jill and her husband Vern to come to supper.

When they arrive, they hardly speak to each other and are barely civil to the rest of us. Every topic I try to discuss is turned around to the subject of the wedding.

"Everything costs too damned much," Vern says. "I don't want to sound cheap, but..."

"*Sound cheap? You are cheap*! If you say one more word, I'll scream!" Jill tells him.

Hanging his head, Vern grumbles, "The groom ain't near good enough for this family. No account. That's all there us to it. I can't hardly stand him."

"One more word! That's more than I can take!"

We eat the rest of the meal in silence. After our dinner, as we clean up the kitchen, Jill fills me in on the folks' medications. She snaps at me when I ask questions, so I decide that Mother is correct about not mentioning her crooked arm. I'll wait to address that issue after the wedding.

Jill and Vern are about to leave when my dad says, "Here, I want you all to see this."

Sitting in his favorite old armchair, he yanks off his house shoes and socks and then pulls up his trouser legs. We gather around and bend over, looking at his feet. His right foot is incredibly swollen. Nearly twice the size of his left one. I've never seen anything like it.

"That must be gout," I say.

"Nope, not gout," he answers.

"When did you notice this?" Vern asks.

"I've had it for several days," Dad answers.

"And you didn't say anything!" my sister shrieks. "Why didn't you tell anyone?"

"I'm telling you now," my dad says, quietly.

"Well, for God's sake, Daddy!"

"Don't talk to your dad that way!" Vern yells.

"I'll be all right! Go on home now. I'll be fine."

"The hell you will!" Jill screams.

"Leave me alone. I'll be just fine," Like my mother, he's a martyr.

"Calm down and shut up!" Vern yells at Jill.

Mother and I sit on the couch in the family room and watch all three of them throw tantrums.

Jill yells, "All right! Don't see a doctor and die! I don't care! I've had all I can take!" She runs out the back door. I notice she's wearing her tennis shoes. Since she's a health nut and runs in races, I figure she won't fall and break her neck running home after dark.

Vern turns red-faced, apparently embarrassed. He

says, "I'll be glad to take you to the doctor in the morning."

"Nope. Not going."

"Well, don't blame me if they have to amputate your foot! I'm outa here!" Vern walks out, banging the door. We hear him zoom off.

Ten minutes later, Vern calls. "Has your sister come back?" he asks. "She's not home. When she ran out of your folks' house, I forgot that we had come together. Anyway, her car is here, but the house is dark, and she's gone."

When Mother hears the Missing Jill news, she panics. "Where could your sister be? Oh, my Lord, what if someone kidnapped her? Or what if she's fallen and broken her leg?

"Calm down, Mother," I say. My Lord, why did I ever leave Memphis?

Vern starts looking for Jill and calls us from his cell phone periodically, reporting that he can't find her. He sounds more distraught with every call.

"Damn!" Dad says. "What's the matter with that woman? *I* didn't cause this!"

"Oh, no?" asks Mother, holding her broken wing. "You old polecat, of course you did. You're completely responsible!"

The phone rings again. This time it's the sheriff. "We've picked up your sister," he tells me, "way out past Cemetery Road. She was running through a pasture, and a farmer thought she was an intruder. Lucky, he didn't shoot her. We'll bring her to your house. Your folks' house, that is."

My sister, the choir director of the First Methodist Church, run down by the Law.

"Why not take her to her own home?" I ask.

"She's mad at her husband and wants to come there. She's crying a lot. I think we should do what she says."

Oh, goody. I call Vern and tell him the good news. "Not abducted, not raped and not murdered. Just crazy. And mad as hell at you."

Jill and the sheriff arrive at the front door at the same time Vern walks in the back. Immediately after depositing Jill, the sheriff departs. This time, Mother, Daddy and I watch simultaneous grief, anger, tears and recriminations, presented by the parents of the bride. Finally, his house shoes and socks back on, my dad stands.

"Enough," he says. "It's time for ya'll to get home. I'll walk you to your car." He limps out, and they follow. Leaving Mother on the couch, I trail along behind.

"So sorry, so sorry," Jill weeps.

"She's all worked up about the damned wedding," Vern explains.

The idiot makes me glad I don't have a husband.

Jill climbs into the passenger's side of the front seat and pulls the door toward her. Unfortunately, my dad's left hand is holding onto the inside of the car door frame, and the heavy door smashes it.

"Damn!" he yells. "Son of a bitch!" He pulls the door back.

Jill shrieks, loud and long.

The fleshy part of Dad's hand is squashed. Blood rapidly rises through the thin old skin, and I run into the house to get towels for him.

"Please leave," I say to my sister, wrapping the injury. "Let me take care of this."

"Are you crazy?" she screams. "We have to take him to the hospital!"

"I can do that," I tell her. "I did this a million times when I worked at the Y. I know just what to do." I hustle my dad into my vehicle. "You go inside and tell Mother," I say to Jill. "I'll take care of Dad."

"I'll go with you," Vern says.

"Oh, no you won't," I answer, starting the ignition. "Stay with your wife. Try to keep her from killing somebody."

Fortunately, no one in this small West Texas town has been shot or suffered a heart attack in the last hour, and there are no patients in the emergency room. My dad and I see the doctor immediately.

And luckily, no bones are broken. A tetanus shot, a pain killing shot, a dozen stitches and a bandage later, I say, "Dad, while we're here, show the doctor your swollen foot."

"I really don't want to," he says.

"Do it!" I order.

The emergency room doctor has stitched Daddy up without a change of expression. But when he sees the swollen foot, he says, "This is serious. Really serious. I want you to spend the night here, so I can get tests started on you early in the morning. It'll be a good thing, because this way we can control your pain."

"I'm in no pain," Daddy says.

"You will be when the shot wears off," the doctor assures him. "I want you to stay the night here."

"Dad, please cooperate."

"I'll cooperate, but I need to go home first."

"I can bring you anything you need."

"No, you can't. Take me home." He looks at the doctor. "I'll be back."

Furious, I drive him home. "Here we are. Now what's so all-fired important that it can't wait until morning?"

I'm not going to that hospital without some bourbon," he says. "Get it for me, in the pantry. Pack it in my bag with my pajamas and a *National Geographic*, and I'll go back."

"You can't take liquor into a hospital!"

"I can, and I will," he says.

Mother has pulled off her clothes, hung them up, and put on her nightgown. She's rubbing cold cream into her face, sitting in front of the television set, watching CNN.

Oh, dear John, what is it now?" she asks, as I walk through the room carrying a small suitcase. Daddy follows close behind, but he isn't talking to either of us.

"Don't worry, Mother. I have this under control." I tell her about Daddy going to the hospital.

"Where does he hide his liquor?" I ask.

"He has a hundred hiding places. Start looking in the kitchen, under the sink or in the cabinet above the oven."

Bingo! I find an unopened pint of bourbon in the second place I look, above the oven. All my life my dad has played this game. Hide the liquor and nobody will ever know that you drink. Nobody could ever suspect by your behavior, your demeanor, your language, your red face, or your whiskey breath.

I put the bourbon, shaving kit, pajamas and the newspaper into the small roll-on. Then I put Mother to bed.

Finally, I drive Daddy back to the emergency room. Slowly, I get him admitted. So many questions, most of which he refuses to answer. At last, a nurse takes us to his room, where we get him into bed. All of those things accomplished, the nurse leaves the room. I walk over to kiss him goodnight.

"Aren't you forgetting something?" he asks.

"What?"

"A Coke. And a glass of ice."

It takes a long time to find the correct change for the Coke machine. Then I order ice from the kitchen, which causes hostility from the staff.

"I'm worried about leaving Mother for so long," I say.

"She's asleep by now," he says. "I expect you to take care of things for me, and then you can go."

It's nearly midnight when I leave my father, sitting in his hospital bed in the semi-darkness, sipping a strong bourbon and Coke. He's in a perfectly good mood.

At the end of the hall, I stop by the nurses' station.

"You might check on my dad," I tell them. "He might be drinking something he shouldn't." Leaving quickly, I try not to think about what I've done.

"Phlebitis," the doctor says, the next day. "It's the inflammation of a vein. Can be dangerous, but your dad should respond well to the medication."

"When can he come home?"

"I want him to stay with us for a few days," the doctor answers.

"We have a wedding this weekend," I say. "His only grandchild."

"We'll see how he gets along," the doctor says and smiles. Not reassuring at all.

After the doctor leaves, Dad looks at me. "Don't think you're going to get rid of me by locking me up in this damned hospital."

"Oh, Daddy, don't be ridiculous!"

"Last night after you left, that old warthog nurse came in here and snatched my drink. Then she looked through my suitcase and found my bottle of bourbon. I thought you'd hidden it!"

"It's probably just as well, Daddy. You really shouldn't be drinking in here anyway. The nurses must monitor your intake and output. They need to know what you're consuming."

"You'd better bring me some more bourbon."

"No, I'm not going to."

I take Mother to the beauty shop. She's planned to host the bridesmaid's luncheon in two days, the day of the wedding, with me serving as the major caterer. I'm certain she'll change her plans now.

"Let's have the bridesmaids come for lunch at Marabelle's Tearoom," I tell her. "It's a darling place. A few phone calls and *Voila!* The party will be arranged like magic."

"The girls are coming to my house," she says. "I've already invited them."

"We can change it, Mother. We won't be changing anything about the party except the place."

"You promised to prepare the meal! And serve it!"

"That was before I saw your arm. And before Jill went berserk and took off on a running rampage. And before Dad was hospitalized with a serious circulatory condition!"

"We're having that luncheon! I won't let Emily down. Besides, it won't be any trouble."

I drive down Main Street, seriously tempted to run the car up on the sidewalk, through the First National Bank plate glass window.

"Take me home now," she orders. "I have everything arranged and organized. Everything's been done. You won't have to do a damned thing except prepare the meal, make the rice bags, and arrange the centerpieces."

"How many rice bags?"

"Oh, quite a few. Your sisters invited everybody in town."

"Good grief, Mother. I'm not Superwoman."

"Billie Doris will help. She's done all the other work already."

"I thought that Billie Doris was on dialysis!"

"She is, but she doesn't go for a treatment every day!"

Billie Doris Ramsey, the African American woman who has helped my mother for decades, is old and sick. If she's my major helper, I'm in trouble. Driving home, I look at Mother and wonder when she became so crazy.

Then I notice the car in front of me turning into my parents' driveway. Curious, I pull up to the curb in front of their house. Mother notices the car also.

It's a taxi. The driver gets out, walks around the automobile, and opens the back door. Dad climbs out. The driver pulls Daddy's suitcase out of the trunk, and Daddy gives him a couple of bills. After the driver backs out, Daddy sees us. He grabs his bag and hightails it to the front door, but I'm too quick for him.

"What are you doing? You know you're not supposed to be here! The doctor said you have to stay off your feet!"

"They released me," he says. "I'm not sick after all. Allergies, that's it."

"Oh, Daddy, for Pete's sake," I say, unlocking the door.

Inside, the phone is ringing. It's the hospital. My dad has run away, and everyone is frantic. I assure them that I'll bring him back.

Mother wanders around. I don't know what she's taken, but she is definitely in la-la land. "I'm ready to talk about our party," she says.

"Not now, Mother, I've got a problem with Dad."

"What are you doing home, you old geezer?" my mother asks him.

"Where do you keep your bourbon?" I ask him.

"I don't know," he looks at Mother. "There might be some in the garage."

"Hidden where?"

"Not hidden. But maybe behind the blood and bone meal."

"I'm going to fix you a stiff drink. As strong and as large as you want. But just one. Then you're getting into my car. If I have to, I'll call Billie Doris's husband Vick to carry you. I'm taking you back to the hospital."

"Not without my bottle of bourbon."

"OK, I'll take a damned bottle of bourbon, too."

"But this time, you won't tell that old bitch nurse."

"Right. I won't tell a soul."

When I get my dad good and snockered, he's easy to manage, but the afternoon is half gone, and my mother is pouting.

"Hurry up with him," she says, "because you and I have work to do!"

I take him back to the hospital, install him in his room, and hide his liquor in a plastic Wal-Mart sack behind his newspapers in the nightstand.

On my way out, I tell the nurse, "He hates taking orders from anybody."

"We may have to restrain him," she says.

"I hope not."

"Does he have any liquor this time?" she asks.

"I wouldn't think so. You confiscated it, didn't you?" I ask.

It's late afternoon by the time I return home, and I immediately start making the rice bags.

The next day, Billie Doris comes early to help. Working like mad, we prepare all the food, set up the luncheon tables, and finish stuffing and tying over 400 rice bags. Mother sits with her elbow on the kitchen table, her arm reaching upward, fingers waving. She watches us and gives orders.

My sister, hysterical and needing a Valium, rushes in and out of the house all day.

"That woman sure do a lot of skittering," says Billie Doris.

"Yep," I reply. "*Skittering* is the right word for it."

Then on the next day Billie Doris, who suffered a bad night and doesn't feel much like helping, comes to work anyway, out of a fanatical loyalty to Mother. The two old ladies sit on the sofa as I arrange flowers for six centerpieces and then set the tables. Then Billie Doris helps Mother dress, while I throw on some decent clothes and arrange a fake smile on my face.

The bridesmaids arrive at noon. Silly, spoiled, and shallow, my niece, Emily, has no idea what trouble she's caused. My beautiful zombie-eyed mother is a relaxed, charming hostess, my crazed sister has taken a tranquilizer, Billie Doris and I work well together as servers, and the luncheon is a success. Soon it's time for our guests to go home and dress for the wedding.

While Billie Doris finishes cleaning up, I zip out to the hospital to check on my dad. This is not an amusing sight. He sits, morose, in his dimly lighted room, with the sports channel blaring on the television. He lifts his blanket and shows me that the nursing staff has tied him to his bed with a wide canvas belt around his waist.

"Oh, Daddy, I'm so sorry," I tell him.

"I'm going to miss my granddaughter's wedding," he says.

"But you're so sick, you really wouldn't enjoy it."

"Miss all the fun."

"I'm not sure it's going to be all that much fun," I say.

"You're just trying to make me feel better," he answers. "Everybody in town will be there. Everybody but me."

When I arrive back at my parents' home, I put the finishing touches on Mother, and then I dress. We arrive at the church in plenty of time, and she radiantly stands with the others and has her picture taken. No one mentions Daddy.

We sit in the sanctuary, the setting sun shining through the rose window above the chancel. The soloist stands and sings, "Wind Beneath My Wings." As I listen to the lyrics, I think about how people hold each other up. I realize that my sister has propped my parents up until she herself is practically crazy. I wonder who will ultimately be there to prop me up when it becomes necessary. With no husband, no children, and no prospective long-term boyfriend, my old-age future looks grim. Not happy thoughts, just before Emily's wedding.

Wearing an assortment of brightly colored gowns in

hues matching the stained-glass window, the bridesmaids float down the aisle. Clothes, flowers and music are perfectly planned and exactly what Emily wanted. The wedding is a work of art.

Some movement to my left distracts me, and I turn my head. Through the aisle window, I see Daddy, dressed in his Sunday suit, climbing out of the same taxi he used for his hospital escape two days ago. He hobbles up the sidewalk to the church.

I can't trust him, so I slip to the end of the pew and up the side aisle to the foyer, just in time to catch him as he enters the church. The bridesmaids still slowly move into the sanctuary.

"What's the matter with you?" I grab him.

"Damn! I'm coming to my granddaughter's wedding!"

"How did you get away?" I whisper.

"That stupid old warthog nurse. I asked her for scissors to trim my moustache. It took me a long time to cut that restraining belt. After that, I called the cab."

I picture him, cutting at that tough strap for most of the day, hiding it from me, and then calling the taxi. I imagine him sneaking away, going home and dressing in his best suit, determined to join the festivities.

He's shaky, sick and limping. "I'm glad you're here." I hug him.

"Me, too," he answers. 'No one likes to feel left out."

As I lead Daddy down the side aisle, the bridesmaids continue to process. When we come to the grandparent pew, Daddy stops, always the gentleman, and lets me enter first. Then we move in together, and I sit between him and my mother.

Leaning over, Mother reaches across me and pats his knee. "How'd you get away, you sly old fox?" she asks, smiling.

"Gave the nurse the slip," he whispers, putting his hand over hers.

The last bridesmaid, the seventh, reaches the altar. The girls' richly colored dresses perfectly match the brilliant stained-glass window – red, orange, yellow, green, blue, indigo, and violet. The colors of the rainbow, symbol of hope, a metaphor for God's promise. The music swells with the chords of "Lohengrin," and the minister motions for everyone to rise. Standing, we turn to watch the beautiful bride, escorted by her perspiring father.

"All right, Emily, honey!" Dad yells unsteady on his feet and smelling of bourbon. "The wedding's on! Let 'er rip!"

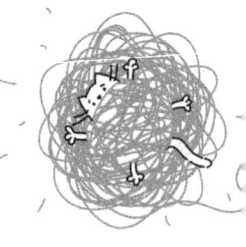

THE ELEPHANT MOUND

When Dr. Clarence Rally became president of picturesque Mountainview College, he inherited a campus with over a one-hundred-year-old history. The school was in the pre-Civil War town of Rennieville, Arkansas, in the lush green foothills of the Ozark Mountains.

On top of the town's most sizeable hill stood a classical building which was once a large Presbyterian Church. During the war, this church had served both as a hospital and as a lookout point for the Confederate Army. Now it was the administration building for the college. When Rally took over the presidency, this church/hospital/administration and classroom building was practically falling down.

One of Rally's main objectives, his board of trustees told him, was to modernize the old campus. All the buildings were dilapidated. All were filled with outdated plumbing, peeling walls, uneven floors, leaking roofs and rattling windows.

Although charming, the place was falling apart.

Dr. Rally was a middle-aged, medium-sized, grey-haired man with enthusiasm and energy. Work was his main interest. He dressed in suits and ties and had few clothes for leisure. His wife, Lucy, was short, blond and always dressed elegantly. She was as enthusiastic as her husband. Add to that, she was a bit on the dramatic side, which was natural, since she was a drama major at State University. She had honed her skills by playing Lady Macbeth in both high school and college.

Despite its decrepitude, the campus was in a gorgeous setting. In the spring, dogwoods, redbud trees and jonquils flourished. In summer, huge oaks spread their leafy limbs throughout the area, and wildflowers danced along the roads. In autumn, every tree and shrub were a blaze of red and orange glory. In winter, all was drab except the tall evergreens that seemed to protect the territory. But when it snowed, the entire area looked like a Christmas card.

Inspired by the beautiful natural setting of the campus, as well as the expectations of the school's board of trustees, Dr. Rally went to work. Along with Lucy, as well as with his influential and wealthy trustees, he was able to replace or renovate the major campus buildings within five years. Enrollment went up and the quality of the faculty improved. The trustees were pleased, and they gave the president an impressive raise.

"I'm exhausted," Dr. Rally told Lucy one night after a board meeting. "But before I retire, I'm determined to build a new library for the college."

Lucy agreed. And as a result of his suggestion, the trustees were so enthusiastic about a modern library that they raised the money very quickly. Then, after conferring with architects, it was decided the library should be built in the center of the campus, in a wide expanse called by the locals "The Elephant Mound."

No one on campus knew why the grassy area had such a strange name. Dr. Rally could not find any reference to it in the notes of past presidents. So, Lucy Rally planned a tea party and invited eight of the staunchest local church ladies and supporters of the college. Lucy knew that these ladies had grown up in Rennieville. They would know the story.

Hauling out the presidential china, silver, crystal, and linens, Lucy served tiny cookies, tea from an elaborate silver pot, and delicious mimosas from a cut-glass pitcher. She had been careful not to invite Baptists or members of the Church of Christ, who would be offended by even a hint of liquor. But Lucy knew that mimosas can get ladies to talk.

None of the guests were in the mood for tea; all preferred the mimosas. They chatted in the Rally's living room, each one becoming happier by the minute.

When Lucy asked about Elephant Mound, her guests told her the story of Sapphire, the elephant.

Although they had been children at the time, these elderly women vividly remembered the burial of Sapphire. The actual event occurred decades ago, in the early thirties. The president of the college was Dr. Wesley, a Presbyterian minister. While he was away, soliciting funds from New York donors, a circus came to town. And with the circus was an elderly elephant named Sapphire. She was too feeble to do her circus tricks and would likely die any day. So, the circus manager decided to leave Sapphire with the college. He reasoned that the biology department could take her in and after her death, the students could dissect and study her.

The students and the professors in the biology department were thrilled with the possibilities that lay ahead. The head of that department accepted the elephant and tied her to a maple tree near the center of the campus, in a large space between the old science building and the unfinished construction of a new chapel.

If Sapphire had been in her prime, she could have easily uprooted the tree, but she was too sick to care.

A few days later, when Dr. Wesley returned, he announced he had been successful in raising enough money not only to save the school but also to finish building the chapel. But his joy was diminished by the presence of the dying elephant.

The very next day, school children and town residents came to the campus to see old Sapphire. Children wept openly, and adults clenched their jaws, bowed their heads, and sighed. All left with tears in their eyes.

"Oh, it was awful!" one of Lucy's guests exclaimed. "Sapphire was so sad, she looked like she was crying. People brought her hay and water, but she wouldn't eat or drink anything. Everybody in town was upset."

"I was just a little girl," said another. "We could hear her breathing all over town. Even at night, when I went to bed, I could hear old Sapphire."

The women jabbered at once.

"Everybody was sad. Word was that Dr. Wesley called the biology professors into his office and gave them the dickens."

"They had their knives and scalpels ready, just waiting to dissect the poor animal."

"But he told them they couldn't do it. Too upsetting. People were already grieving for her. If the professors performed scientific experiments on the elephant, people would hate them and the college as well."

"Scalpels and knives!" exclaimed another, as she wiped her eyes with Lucy's linen napkin.

Lucy poured another round. "So, what happened next?" she asked.

"Dr. Wesley called the members of the science department into his office and told them they were responsible for what he called *the elephant crisis*. They should never have accepted Sapphire in his absence. He would not allow them to dissect her. He was so angry he put them in charge of digging the elephant's grave."

"Oh, yes, Dr. Wesley was quite firm about it. He told the science teachers they would dissect Sapphire over his dead body!"

"All the students helped dig the grave — the boys, not the girls, of course. But the girls helped prepare food and drinks for the workers and some were strong enough to wheelbarrow the dirt away. Dr. Wesley had to cancel classes in order to get all the work done."

"Because Sapphire was dying mighty fast."

"I remember asking the Lord to save Sapphire," one guest sighed.

"Oh, we all did."

"Pretty soon Sapphire died, and everybody thanked Dr. Wesley for his foresight about the burial."

Lucy asked, "And then what happened?"

"Oh, by then her grave was ready."

"The mayor dismissed school on the day of the burial. All the schoolchildren lined up to watch. Dr. Wesley even said a prayer. It took eight mules and every heavy rope in the county to pull her into the hole. Then the college boys covered her up."

"Ever since then that mound in the center of the campus has been known as the grave of Sapphire."

"That's why the grass is so green on the campus. We owe it all to her."

"Over seventy years ago," said another. "And yet, I remember it well."

Lucy loved these dear sweet women and didn't want to cause any distress. Still, she decided that she should be the one to tell them.

"Will you be upset if a new library is built on top of Sapphire's grave?"

"Oh, heavens no!" they exclaimed. They all agreed a center of learning resting on dear old Sapphire would be appropriate.

"But in order to pour a foundation, they'll have to dig her up," said one lady, sipping her third mimosa.

"And of course, the building will need a basement," said another. "So, they'll dig pretty deep."

"Surely, even after all this time, they'll find her skeleton — or part of it." said a third.

"Oh, of course they will!" the ladies all agreed.

"And won't that be ironic?" one of them said, as she glanced at Lucy. "It looks like the science department will win the battle over Sapphire after all."

"How so?" asked Lucy.

"They'll get to study her bones."

"Let's drink a toast to Sapphire the elephant," Lucy said, as she stood and poured another round of mimosas. "She was a beloved creature. I'll ask Clarence to name one of the rooms in the library after her. And if we can find her picture, we'll frame it and hang it at the entrance."

"Hear, hear!" The guests lifted their wobbling glasses. "Let's drink to that poor old dead elephant!"

"And let's drink to the marvelous new library!" added the wily Lucy Rally.

"Hear, hear!" they all cried. "Hear, hear!"

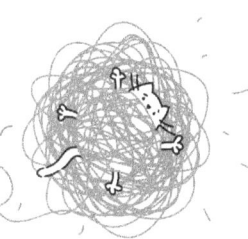

A STORY OF AN HOUR

"Just quit your bitchin' and let me drive," college president Clarence Rally growled at his wife, Lucy, as he turned left on a one-way street marked, "No Left Turn."

"Your attitude is irritating beyond belief," she snapped. Car horns blared at them. "Do you want to get us killed?"

Like a race car driver, President Rally hunkered down over the steering wheel. "What I want is for you to stop nagging," he growled again.

"Then for God's sake, pay attention! You've got to get off this street!"

"And you've got to get off my back!"

"Well, why in God's name did you give me the map and ask for directions? You've ignored everything I've said!"

Dr. Rally was silent. He swung off the one-way street and drove to the next one, turning left again. Then he asked, "How far is it now to Commerce Street?"

"If you're so goddamn smart, you can find Commerce yourself!" Lucy resolved not to say another word.

For this I pulled myself out of bed before dawn. For this I nearly broke my neck yesterday to book a hair appointment and a manicure. For this I shopped for a month for a new navy-blue suit. For this I pulled on pantyhose before one single rooster in the state of Arkansas crowed, damn him!

Dr. Clarence Rally, President of Mountainview College in Rennieville, Arkansas, and his lovely wife, Lucy, had been invited to a brunch at the Little Rock Golf and Country Club, honoring long-time donor and lifetime trustee of the college, Farrell Faragut. They were pleased to have been included in the guest list and had arisen early and driven down the steep narrow roads to Little Rock. Dr. Rally had planned to arrive early—in time for a short private congratulatory word with Mr. Faragut. But he had miscalculated, and they were about to be late. Now this! Construction on the streets. Dr. Rally concentrated on his driving.

He reminded his wife more and more of Walter Mitty. "Insufferable son of a bitch," Lucy hissed. *There, that's it—that is all I have to say. I won't say another word.*

If she had a gun, she would shoot her husband. *"Lord, please make Congress pass a tough gun control law,"* she prayed silently. *"Because if I had a gun, I might spend the rest of my life in jail."*

Lucy crossed her arms over her chest, looked out the window, and began mentally composing newspaper headlines:

COLLEGE PRESIDENT'S WIFE GOES BERSERK

FRIENDS SAY NO WARNING FOR WOMAN'S RAMPAGE

RENNIEVILLE IN SHOCK

WIFE COULD NOT STAND ONE MORE SMART ALECK, SARCASTIC REMARK *No, that one is too complicated,* Lucy decided. *Let's just keep it simple.*

WIFE SHOOTS HUSBAND OVER TRAFFIC DIRECTIONS

I don't know if I'd really shoot to kill, mused Lucy. *Just maim him a little. I'd like to make him really, really sorry for being such a sanctimonious shit.*

WOUNDED HUSBAND APOLOGIZES

LUCY STRIKES BLOW FOR ALL WOMEN WITH A MAP. *No, too long, too wordy. Keep it short. Succinct.*

Lucy settled into her martyr role. To become the wife of a college president, she had made great sacrifices. She rolled them over in her mind. *I gave up a law practice in Texas—where attorneys not only are paid well but also are held in high esteem. Well, not really. But I actually might have become a lawyer, if it had occurred to me, and if my grades had been good enough, and if I had been interested in legal issues.*

What else had she sacrificed? *I gave up a lucrative career in advertising. With my creative eye, I could have made a mint of money. Or I might have become an interior designer. Or I could have been a pediatric surgeon, operating on poor sick children all over the world. However, working on babies is an immense responsibility. Maybe I should have been a veterinarian. Dogs and cats can be pretty damned interesting. And if occasionally one of my patients died, I wouldn't grieve forever.*

I could have been a writer, an actress, maybe even a realtor. Or I might have become a college president. The potential was there, the possibilities endless. And maybe it's not too late.

I've gotten bogged down with this arrogant man who snaps at me when he clearly doesn't know what the hell he's doing or where the hell he's going.

Lucy resolved not to speak to him again for the rest of her life. If they survived the trip, she would hire a lawyer who could serve him papers. She would be out of Dodge on the next train to Dixie. Free, at last, free at last. How did it go? *Thank God Almighty, I'm free at last.* Lucy smiled.

"What I don't understand," she said, "is why you insisted that I come with you today. Since you're such a big-shot and don't need me."

Dr. Rally said nothing. He kept driving south, slowing the car at each intersection, peering up at each street sign.

Lucy resolved never, *ever* to speak to him again.

He turned right on Commerce. He drove east for several blocks and then turned right again.

What the hell is he doing?

For no reason she could determine, they were back at the corner where their troubles had begun.

This is a nightmare. This can't be real! I think I hear Twilight Zone music.

Once again, Dr. Rally turned left. Horns honked, as he

drove into oncoming traffic. Lucy drew a deep breath and waited for her life to flash before her eyes. Instead, flashing lights in her right-hand mirror caught her attention. Then she heard the siren.

"Well, I'll be a son of a bitch," muttered Dr. Rally. He pulled the car over to the curb and waited. The officer appeared to be twelve years old. At the cop's request, Dr. Rally got out of the car, and Lucy saw him pull his billfold from his right hip pocket. His face had turned a ghastly shade of gray, and he looked pathetic. Watching the two men, Lucy waited for a long time. She decided that her husband was not well.

What if he suddenly keels over?

COLLEGE PRESIDENT SUFFERS STROKE OVER TRAFFIC TICKET

LOST COLLEGE OFFICIAL HAS HEART ATTACK, DIES

ARKANSAS TOWN IN MOURNING

WIFE AND COP HELPLESS TO SAVE HUSBAND

When her husband climbed back into the driver's seat, Lucy reached over and patted his shoulder. "Are you all right?"

But Dr. Rally acted as if she were not there. Slowly he swung around and headed in the opposite direction. Then he said, "You'll have to help me find my way."

Lucy looked at him carefully. Once more, she patted his shoulder. "I'll be glad to help, you silly old man."

Ten minutes later, they pulled into Valet Parking at the Little Rock Golf and Country Club. She checked her lipstick, and he straightened his tie. Together they marched through the door of the reception room and immediately they embraced Farrell Faragut. Then they went into their old never-fail mix-and-mingle routine. To the other guests, President Rally handed out hearty slaps on the back, gentlemanly bows, and warm handshakes, as the first lady gave tittering giggles, hugs and kisses. What a handsome, happy, loving couple they were.

Everyone agreed.

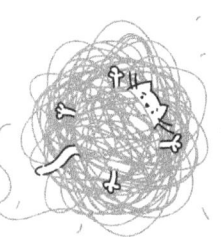

THE PIG MAN

She was one of those brilliant women—an excellent researcher and an extraordinary writer—who saturate the campuses of colleges and universities throughout the country. With a Ph.D. in English literature—specializing in the eroticism of D. H. Lawrence in art and fiction—she found that even a bright inquisitive mind and laudable teaching skills could not land her a full-time position in a major university.

She had tried. From the spring semester when she had graduated and concurrently published her dissertation, she had sent out *resume* after *resume*. She practically memorized the Faculty Positions section of *The Chronicle of Higher Education*, firing away letters and inquiries. Finally, she hired a headhunter. Unfortunately, too many qualified English professors competed for very few positions.

So, for years she worked in New York City—teaching as an adjunct faculty member in three colleges simultaneously—riding the subway to and from each school and then back to the apartment that she shared with her two sisters. Rising early, packing up corrected student essays, an apple and a sandwich in the same briefcase that her father, a humanities professor, had carried, she tied on tennis shoes and wrapped her brown leather purse around her neck and shoulder. Her routine consisted of teaching, grading, preparing assignments each semester, and then quickly forgetting each student. She was quite sure that they forgot her, also.

She knew that she was not attractive. Once in an essay a student had described her as short and dumpy, which came as no surprise. She knew that her face was square, that her hands and feet were short and wide, that she wore loose fitting colorless clothes. She knew that other women sparkled, but for some reason she did not. She wondered if she washed her hair often enough and wondered if her clothes were really clean. But she refused to discuss the subjects of health or personal hygiene with her sisters.

She was nearing forty. She had no full-time employment, no pension, no retirement plan, no savings, no health insurance. She had never had an office. Oftentimes, after an evening of beer and a movie with friends, she awoke in the night, quite frightened.

She realized that she must aggressively work to change her career. She decided to stop sending out her *resume* to the major schools, so the spring semester of her tenth year of teaching she applied instead to twenty-five colleges on a somewhat lower level of academic acclaim. Nothing happened. She was not granted a single interview. She began to lie awake at night, wondering what had happened to her dreams.

The next year she decided to send her resume to every institution that indicated any possible opening for a person with anything close to her qualifications. She received one invitation for an interview. She flew to Little Rock, Arkansas, rented an automobile, and drove north up the torturous highway into the Ozark Mountains to Mountainview College in Rennieville, population 6,000. Her interview lasted for two days. About a week after she had returned to New York City, the Dean of the Mountainview College called her and offered her a teaching position.

She moved to Rennieville in August. She rented a small house with a fenced-in backyard and began a new life. She thought that she would die of loneliness. It had never occurred to her that she would miss her sisters so dreadfully.

Within a month after school began, her office suitemate brought her a large short-haired spotted mongrel that someone had abandoned on the highway. She cleaned him up and named him Ernest Hemingway. A few weeks later, upon leaving the grocery store, she spied another stray, sniffing around a dumpster. She took the small tan dog home, bathed and fed her. She named the new dog Pauline.

She spent her evenings grading papers and preparing lectures. Every night at 10 o'clock she sat on her secondhand sofa between her dogs and watched the news. Every morning she laced up her tennis shoes, put her papers, her apple and her sandwich into her briefcase, and walked from her house up the hill to the campus, where she spent the day.

Every weekend she washed her hair, bought groceries, and read a novel. Every Sunday evening, she called her sisters. She told them that she had nobody, only the dogs.

Every week they told her, "You must get out and meet people!"

"You must make an effort!"

"You should ask some people over for dinner!"

"You must go to the movies!"

"You should get involved in something—something off campus!"

"You could take up a sport—maybe golf or tennis!"

"You should put those dogs on a leash and go out walking!"

"For God's sake, join the church!"

"For God's sake, take up a hobby!"

"For God's sake, volunteer for some committee work!"

"Why don't you have a make-over?"

"Why don't you buy some new clothes?"

"Why don't you just go shopping?"

"Remember that you'll soon be coming home for Christmas."

"Remember that the semester is almost over!"

"Remember that we'll see each other soon."

"Remember that you're not the first woman to live alone."

"Remember that you're not the first person in the world to be miserable."

Every Sunday night after telephoning her sisters she would lie in bed on her back—with Pauline by her side and Ernest at her feet. She looked up at the dark ceiling and felt tears running down the sides of her face.

"I wonder if this is how it feels to be in a bell jar," she asked herself again and again.

During her Christmas vacation, she spent over three weeks in New York City. She decided that most of all she had missed the loud city noises: the dissonant traffic, the screaming voices, the variety of accents, the honking of horns, the raucous rap music from someone's boombox. She walked Manhattan streets, alone or with friends, absorbing the sounds of the city, storing them up to replay later, while she was alone with her dogs in her Ozarks kitchen.

One day she told her sisters, "You have no idea how deadly quiet it is in a small Southern town. In my house there is no noise at all. The telephone almost never rings. And when it does, I can be sure that it is either a telemarketer or a wrong number. Believe me, you have not lived—or died—until you've spent time by yourself in small town America."

Her sisters suggested that she put herself on a health/fitness/beauty regimen when she returned to Arkansas. She had told them about the beautiful women in her classes.

"You would be amazed at how beautiful they all are. They are incredibly tall and tan and thin. They have either blond streaky hair or else luscious long dark curls. Most of them are sorority women, and most of them have won at least one beauty contest. I have never seen anything like it."

"So, your women students are beautiful—but are they smart?"

"Their intelligence does not seem to be of great significance."

"You should look at this experience as a great adventure in your long brilliant career."

Thus, day after day, the college professor received advice and encouragement from her sisters.

After Christmas in New York she believed that she was in better shape. She returned to Rennieville in a cheerful mood. The dogs had spent the holiday with her colleague, who lived out in the mountainous countryside, but they were ecstatic to be with her in their own house and yard once again. She settled back and began preparing for the new semester. After all, she had her dogs, a nice house, and a good job. She told herself that she would be happy. She promised herself to work on self-improvement, to lose weight, to exercise. She promised herself to give up the heavy weeping.

He sat at the back of the room in her American literature class. It was the first class of the new semester, and she noticed him immediately. He watched her intently, and his piercing blue eyes never left her face. His mouth wore a twisted smile, and he nodded at her from time to time, as if they shared a delicious secret.

He looked familiar, but she had never seen him before

in her life. Of that she was quite sure. She could not find his name on the roster that the Registrar's Office had sent her. After class, he waited until the other students had left, and then he came up to her desk and explained that he had enrolled late and that his name would be sent to her as a late enrollee. His name was Randall Smythe. He wore jeans, a chambray shirt, a trench coat and cowboy boots. She noticed dark hair at his throat. He offered to help her with her books. He was painfully polite.

He was an older student, and from the first day, he always sat behind the others and he never spoke in class. But after each class he would hang around, engaging her in conversation. His eyes were as bright as cool blue stones. He watched her face and smiled his off-beat one-sided grin. He watched her lips and watched her eyes and forced parts of her to come alive.

He made her laugh. He was somewhat sophisticated and infinitely more interesting than the other students.

One day he explained to her, "You know, I have spent several years in the service. After that, I was in the oil business, and I have traveled all over the world."

He was a small man but several inches taller than she. They walked down the hall together after class, and he began to visit her office nearly every day. He brought her an Arkansas lucky buckeye, a shamrock plant, and once even a basket of Chinese fortune cookies. She could not get over how intently he watched her face.

She imagined that they could discuss practically any subject. One day she told him about going to see the

Rockettes at the Radio City Music Hall every Christmas. "But of course," she added, "my favorite performances are by the New York City Ballet Company."

Her student told her, "My first wife was a ballerina, so I have seen the NYC Ballet Company many times."

"Oh, I did not realize that you had been married."

"Yes, my first wife was killed in a traffic accident. I nearly lost my mind with grief."

With increasing intensity, the college professor looked forward to the conversations with her older student. She told her sisters about him and they were happy that she had found a friend.

One day Randall Smythe came to her office and his face was wild with excitement.

"Would you like for me to bring you a pygmy pig?" he asked. Before she could answer, he explained, "I have a good friend who raises them, and I can get one for you free."

"Well, I don't know. How large would it get? Do they get along with dogs?"

"The pig's parents are small. In fact, the mother weighs only twenty pounds and the father is not much bigger than that. The mother is pregnant, and the litter should be born in a few weeks."

"What about my dogs?"

"Oh, pygmy pigs and dogs get along just fine. But they get along with cats even better. For some reason other animals really love these little pigs. They feel protective of them."

The college professor was delighted and said, "Yes, I would love to have a pygmy pig. But you will have to teach me how to care for it."

A few weeks later, the professor was shocked to learn that her older student did not do well on tests. She handed back his first test paper and asked him to come into her office. He came immediately after class. He told her that he was out of practice, that his study skills were poor, that he had no time to do the reading. He hung his head and avoided her eyes.

A few days later, he returned to her office. "The pig has been born," he announced. "It is beautiful—a black and white spotted male! Believe me, you will love it. It will be able to leave its mother by the end of the semester."

The professor did not know what to say.

"By the way, the little piglet's name is Prince. But, of course, you can change its name if you want to."

Their conversations after every class continued.

Randall Smythe's term paper was unacceptable. It was filled with misspelled words, grammatical errors and poor development of ideas, and it followed no known format for documentation. The professor called him in for another conference. His smile glittered as he apologized for his shoddy work.

"I am not supposed to talk about this," he said, and looked out her office door, while pulling the lapels of his trench coat up around his ears, "but I have been working with the CIA on a secret project. Consequently, I did not have time to do the writing assignment properly."

"You really must try a little harder to do research correctly," she scolded.

"Oh, by the way," he added, with a smile, "little Prince has a wonderful appetite."

The professor decided to cut Randall Smythe some slack. She showed him how to correct the paper. He watched her face, her eyes, her mouth, and his smile widened. She continued to correct the paper and when she had finished, she realized that she had left nothing for him to do. She held his paper and he reached for it—their hands almost touching. She noticed that his hands were small, white, strong—with coarse black hair growing on each pale finger. The contrast was obscene. She could not take her eyes away. His face was very near hers. His white teeth shone like sharp fangs. Suddenly, she felt chilly.

For the rest of that day she felt uneasy, but she lost herself in her work, and prepared a lecture on Poe's "The Pit and the Pendulum." When she finished, she walked down the hill, home to her dark house, and her dogs.

That night she dreamed about Randall Smythe. In her dream he was huge, overpowering. He wore no clothes, but his skin was covered with heavy black hair-like bristles. He stood above her. His penis, gigantic, hung above her face and swung back and forth, back and forth, like a pendulum. Reaching down, he put his face on the pillow, next to hers. Then he snarled—a guttural, deep-throated growl. She watched his face and head grow larger and then his features changed. He gradually began looking more porcine than human. His nose became a snout.

The snout became a pendulum. The pendulum became a swinging penis.

In her conversations with others, she started referring to her student as The Pig Man. Her colleagues did not know him and had not had him in class, which was unusual, in such a small school. A couple of teachers took her aside and said, "Be very careful. You can never tell about some of these bizarre students these days."

She did not tell anyone about her dream.

The semester continued, and the friendship continued also. The Pig Man brought photographs of Prince and described the piglet's personality and habits in detail.

He told her, "You won't believe it, but my friend is planning to take Prince's parents on a television circus roadshow."

He showed her photographs of the pair, wearing various costumes. In one, Prince's father posed in a tuxedo; the mother wore a blue evening gown and pearls. The mother pig's name was The Duchess; the father was Lancelot.

"Look at this!" the Pig Man would say. "Just look at this!"

The college professor from New York City was enthralled with the wonder of it all.

On the day before the final exam, the Pig Man came to her office. He assured her that he would bring Prince to her house just as soon as the piglet was weaned. He asked her for her address and telephone number, as well as her e-mail address. He asked for her summer teaching schedule.

"Of course," he added, "I would hope to see you before I bring Prince."

His eyes had a hypnotic quality. Without hesitation she wrote down the information that he wanted.

On the next day, the Pig Man stopped by her office after taking his final exam. "I nearly went to sleep while I was taking your test," he said, "because I'm just exhausted. Little Prince has been off his feed, and my friend and I have been afraid we were going to lose him."

"Oh no! What happened?" the professor was alarmed.

"The Duchess has been producing bad milk, and the whole litter was getting malnourished."

"Terrible!"

"But not to worry," the tone of his voice was reassuring. "We stayed up all night feeding the piglets a special formula with little bottles. I'm sure that Prince will be fine." The Pig Man looked into his professor's eyes and grinned his twisted smile.

His final exam was not good, and the professor was extremely disappointed. The bottom of her throat began to hurt. She put the test aside and went home to feed her dogs and to rest her eyes.

She told Ernest and Pauline about Prince. She crouched on the kitchen floor with her dogs and kissed each one passionately.

"You simply must try to understand," she said, "that I need someone new to love." Ernest and Pauline sat on the floor and stared at her with sorrowful eyes. She added, "Thank you for expressing compassion and concern."

And then she said, "I have another surprise for you. I am hoping that the Pig Man will come to live with us also."

All night she lay awake, worrying about the Pig Man. She regretted that he could not construct a decent sentence. She was sick at heart that he could not express his thoughts in prose above a third-grade level.

The next morning, she filled out the Registrar's semester grade report. The name Randall Smythe was not there. Puzzled, the professor squarely printed his name at the bottom of the class roster. Next to his name she printed a large A.

"A small price to pay," she thought, "for a pygmy pig. A small price to pay" she assured herself, "for happiness."

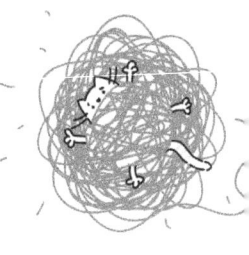

THE CHRISTMAS PARTY SEND-OFF

Pretty Lucy Rally was born to entertain. As the perky first lady of Mountainview College, she was the collegiate Perle Mesta of Arkansas. Heart and soul, she thrust herself into her parties. In the president's mansion, she had plenty of space, employees, dishes, linens, silver and glassware. Plenty of everything except money. So, she had taught herself to be frugal while she entertained lavishly.

And her hard work had paid off. Everyone knew Lucy was her husband's greatest asset, that he would not have wooed donors to the institution without Lucy by his side.

She considered her talents to be gifts from Above. Why else was she blessed with indefatigable energy? She was a gourmet cook, and she could plan a party and seat a hundred people in the Great Room with ease, arrange a dozen centerpieces and execute a delicious banquet, taking into account all diabetic and other dietary restrictions of the guests. Not only was she fulfilling her mission in life with her husband, Clarence, she was serving the Lord in a delightful way.

Lucy's favorite time of year was Christmas. She laid preliminary plans by the first of August. She included guests from the community of Rennieville and towns as far away as Little Rock.

Her parties ranged from the all-school Sunday afternoon Christmas tea for students; the Presbyterian-Methodist ladies' luncheon; the Pan-Hellenic sorority supper; the faculty wives' club Christmas decoration demonstration; the Missionary Baptist ladies' brunch; the faculty children's gingerbread house contest, with a surprise appearance of Santa Claus; the local trustees' Christmas dinner; the music department's Night of Madrigals; the grand and glorious cocktail party for the governor and his wife; numerous small intimate dinner parties for Washington, D. C. politicians who were home for the holidays; and, last but not least, the faculty-staff Christmas cocktail buffet.

Despite all her preparations, she had two major worries, both of which woke her in the middle of the night in a state of cold fear. *What if she threw a party and no one came?* Her other fear was worse. *What if some evening she mistakenly served hard liquor to one of the non-drinking church groups?*

So, Lucy kept menus, copies of invitations, photographs, reminders, and descriptions of the clothing she and her husband wore for each event—down to his choice of holiday necktie.

"The devil is certainly in the details," she told herself.

"And the devil is not going to catch me off guard."

On a cold Monday morning after the school's Thanksgiving break, Lucy walked across campus to go over plans with the manager of the dining room food service. In her briefcase she carried her calendar, sample invitations, guest lists, as well as recipes and pictures of delectable dishes.

"Presentation!" she consistently preached to Brad Hoffman, the campus caterer. "A successful party depends to a great extent on presentation!"

It started to rain. Caught without an umbrella, Lucy ducked into the back door of the Fine Arts Building. Lucy was angry with the Art Department. For the trustees' March meeting, Lucy had planned a *Gone with the Wind* theme. Amid the blooming redbud trees, azaleas, and dogwoods, the faculty-trustee dinner would be held on the veranda of Old Main, the newly restored Administration Building. Flanked by white Grecian columns, the building exuded the charm of an antebellum plantation.

The Art Department had rebelled. Led by Chairman Grant Sherman, they'd refused to attend any of the functions that weekend. They hinted to various members of the board that Mrs. Rally thought she was the reincarnation of Scarlet O'Hara.

Lucy's husband, Dr. Rally, considered the whole thing humorous, but Lucy was furious and determined not to forgive them. So on this particular day, when the sudden rainstorm forced her to walk through the Art Building, she was "as nervous as a porcupine in a roomful of balloons," as her mother would have said.

From the chairman's office, she heard the boorish Sherman's voice, and she caught the words, "President Rally."

Lucy slowed her brisk walk.

"Before long," drawled Sherman, "we'll get those god-awful invitations from the President's wife. It's a shame we can't get out of the faculty-staff Christmas food-fest."

"Are the parties dull?" a faculty member asked.

"Boorrriiinnnggg," drawled Sherman. "But the worst thing —besides the terrible food—is the god-awful punch. Putridly sickening."

"Do we have to go?"

Lucy decided this second speaker must be the new art historian.

"Yeah, unless you break your neck and are dead"

"But President Rally and his wife are nice people, aren't they?"

"*He's* all right. But she walks around with a broomstick up her butt."

Lucy felt hotter than a firecracker. She turned around and marched back to the rear of the building. Her eyes were wet, and her throat ached. So no one would notice her pain, she stood by the backdoor, wearing sunglasses. That bastard in the Art Department had ridiculed her efforts, and she would show *him*. She would have the most lavish faculty Christmas party ever. She would serve scrumptious food and strong, liquored drinks. The whole damned place would be covered with twinkling lights, garlands, wreaths, red velvet bows, and golden gewgaws. There would be games and beautiful music! She would swish around in a new dress and be charming and gracious. She'd give the bastards gifts. And then she would never allow any faculty member—ungrateful sons-of-bitches—to enter the president's mansion again!

In the office of the food manager, she increased the number of trays and dishes, adding a smoked salmon here, a silver tray of caviar there; brandied holiday fruitcakes with champagne-chocolate-strawberry sauce on the side. Elegant tapas would rest on the sideboard, miniature éclairs on the coffee table. Near the grand piano, she'd offer fruity morsels dipped in white chocolate, and a tray of sliced rum cakes, pecan tassies, bourbon balls, divinity, and Aunt Bill's caramel candy in the foyer. A long table of condiments and a delectable smoked turkey in the Great Room. And the *piece de resistance* —a roasted pig with an apple in its mouth in the dining room!

"Using cloves, spell out "Mountainview" across the back end of the pig," she instructed.

"Yes, ma'am," Brad answered.

"Come up with a strong punch recipe. Liven it up. I want the guests to leave our house really, *really* happy."

"And just how happy might that be?"

"Get them snockered on Everclear."

"Mrs. Rally, getting the faculty blind drunk could cost me my job."

Lucy explained that it could only improve their

notoriously sullen attitudes and bring about a festive air. He reminded her that Dr. Rally would never condone such a plan. Lucy retorted that Dr. Rally, himself, could use a strong drink. Finally, they agreed that Brad would mix up a benign white wine punch and that Lucy could add extra liquor if she desired to do so.

Then Lucy zipped across to the printing department to proof the invitations. "I want to add a couple of details," she told Ernie Stubmaster. "At the top, emboss a golden roasted pig and put a red apple in its mouth. And at the bottom, add: 'Bring a wrapped ornament as a gift for the Dirty Santa game.'"

Then Lucy marched to her husband's office. She waved Dr. Rally aside and conferred with his secretary, Cora Greeson, and Cora's student help. "Here is the sample invitation," she said. "And here are the guest lists. Ernie will bring the invitations tomorrow. They must be mailed this week."

At home, Lucy said, "I'm gonna knock 'em dead." She began pulling Christmas decorations from the catacombs of the presidential mansion.

This was a three-story Tudor brick-and-stone built during the boom days of the 1920s. Over 12,000 square feet, it had been built by the Prentiss family of oil well and hog farm fame, on two carefully landscaped acres, containing redbud, magnolia, maple and pine trees, as well as a tennis court, a swimming pool and a fish pond. Perfect for entertaining.

During the first two and a half weeks of December, Dr. and Mrs. Rally held their usual nine holiday events. The climax of the party season would be the faculty-staff gathering on Friday, December 21.

Lucy had made a secret trip to Little Rock and, wearing a knitted cap and sunglasses, had stocked up on Everclear. Then she had purchased a bright red sparkly dress, trimmed with matching feather boa.

"Whoa!" said Dr. Rally when she modeled the outfit for him. She stashed the Everclear beneath the sink in the downstairs powder room, just off the foyer. She added a large, ornate silver pitcher in the cabinet. Her guests would have a smashing evening.

🐾 🐾 🐾

On Thursday morning, Lucy stood in the kitchen in robe and nightgown and answered the telephone.

"I have bad news," her husband said. "Old Tom Lovett died last night."

Tom Lovett had been an eccentric citizen of Rennieville and had been catatonic for the last decade. Old Tom had been the father of Young Tom, a member of the college's board of trustees.

"That's too bad," responded Lucy.

"That's not the bad news," Dr. Rally stammered. "I've agreed to hold the family visitation at our home."

"For God's sake, Clarence! When?"

"Tomorrow evening. We'll have the wake first and then the party."

"The party starts at 7:30! Have you lost your mind?"

"The Lovetts have asked to hold visitation from 5:00 until 7:00. I had to agree. Old Tom has left the school a substantial sum of money."

"Clarence, you're an idiot. Anybody can just hint at giving the school money, and you...."

"Don't be so dramatic. We'll get through this."

"Do the Lovetts know I've got Christmas decorations everywhere?"

"Yes, that's why they requested our home."

"Well, good grief."

President Rally added, "Old Tom's body will arrive tomorrow morning between nine and ten."

"AND WHERE AM I SUPPOSED TO PUT IT?"

"In the library. The family thinks the dark paneling is appropriate for Old Tom."

"And I imagine they want a cozy fire, along with coffee and cookies in the foyer!"

"That would be lovely, dear," he said.

When Lucy hung up, she was shaking. How could her husband put her in such a tizzy? It was his dreadful upbringing! No southern gentleman would be this stupid. Why had she married him? Why, oh why, had she hankered for a Yankee?

She clutched the kitchen counter. "Get a grip, girl," she told herself. "You can't kill or divorce him during the Christmas season. Besides, maybe we *can* pull this off." Lucy poured herself another cup of coffee and went upstairs to dress for the day.

On Friday morning the body arrived. *Pretty snazzy casket*, Lucy thought, as the undertakers wheeled the coffin in and positioned it at the far end of the library. Then they lined the walls in front of the bookcases with floral sprays. When the men started to lift the casket lid, Lucy stopped them.

"If my housekeepers and student servers walk in here and see Old Tom Lovett, they'll run out screaming. Please leave the lid down until the visitation hour."

Dressed in black, one of the twin Hortung brothers of Happy Valley Funeral Home looked at Lucy somberly. "If you wish, Mrs. Rally," he said, bowing. He backed out the door.

At 3:30 p.m. Lucy went upstairs to dress, deciding to wear her old black funeral dress for the visitation. The mourners would leave in time for her to put on the red one. In the mirror, she turned and looked at her backside. "Oh, how I do wish I were thinner," she lamented.

Downstairs, she surreptitiously checked on the Everclear. She poured the first pitcher full and left it beneath the sink. She planned to pour it into the white wine punch at exactly 7:25 p.m.

At 4:30 p.m. the twin Hortungs returned. Toting more flowers, they arranged the coffin and set the lighting in the room to Old Tom's best advantage. Efficiently and mournfully, they moved about, and Lucy expected them to burst into tears.

When Dr. Rally arrived, Lucy said, "Go into the library and observe those two old crows. That'll put you in the mood for a party."

Then the Lovett family was at the front door: about forty people—men, women, and children.

"We know we're a bit early," Melissa Lovett said, "but I wanted everyone to see your house." Immediately, they took off in all directions, examining and praising the president's mansion.

"May I take them upstairs?" Melissa asked. "What about the basement?"

By 5:15 mourners started to arrive. They, too, tromped through the house. Lucy heard them comment, "What gorgeous decorations!"

"Isn't this a beautiful home!"

"Oh, how very elegant!"

"My, don't they have a lot of room!"

"How silly—this great big house for just two people!"

Lucy wondered if they ever went into the library to pay last respects. The coffee and sweets she had set on the table in the foyer were scarfed up, while folks wandered into the living room and beyond that to the garden room, sat down, and made themselves at home. She wondered if people were upstairs in the Rally's private living quarters, looking through closets and drawers.

Soon the food service truck arrived. Expertly, Brad pulled up under the porte-cochere, and his student workers scampered out, laden with pans and trays of party food. Lucy met them in the kitchen.

"We've got a serious problem," she said. "Some

people are here for Old Tom Lovett's funeral visitation. The body is in the library and shows no sign of leaving. I want you to work as quietly as possible, behind closed doors in the dining room and kitchen until I get these people out! If you can possibly hide the food—or leave most of it in the truck — it would be a good idea."

One of the student waiters quipped, "The body is in the library. Colonel Mustard did it with a knife."

Everybody roared except Lucy. "Very funny indeed," she said through lips that did not move.

The mourners continued to swarm the house. Lucy heard a crash from upstairs and a woman's voice, "I told you not to pick that up!" One of the children had broken something, and Lucy dared not go up to look.

At 7:15 the mourners started to trickle away. To keep them from the party food, Lucy had locked the doors to the dining room and kitchen. She had instructed Brad to begin putting food out as soon as he saw the backsides of the Lovetts.

The knotted old Hortung twins attempted to move the mourners along. Finally, they lurked in the foyer like buzzards at either side of the library doorway — tall, dark, gloomy sentries.

Determined to execute her original plan, Lucy ran upstairs to change into the red dress. Quickly she readjusted her face, hair, and bosom. The doorbell rang at exactly 7:30 p.m. She looked at herself in her full-length mirror. She gritted her teeth: "Damn! I look like a fat old harlot!"

Dr. Rally had remained downstairs with the Lovett

family and had no time to change his clothes from the office. But he was appropriately dressed: black suit, black tie, black shoes, and black socks — the ones with gold stitching on the heels. He literally bought these comfortable socks from Wal-Mart by the dozens.

When Lucy descended her pinecone-decorated staircase, Brad was setting out the last tray of hors d'oeuvres. The musicians had arrived and were setting up; the lighting was perfect; and the punchbowl was three quarters full of Brad's bland white wine concoction. Brad was busy and her husband was greeting guests. Lucy slipped into the powder room and emerged with the silver pitcher, the contents of which she dumped into the punch bowl. Lucy smiled as she began to serve.

In a few moments, Dr. Rally sidled up to her. "I have some bad news," he said, under his breath. "We need to keep everybody out of the library. Old Tom is still in there. The guests were arriving, so I asked the Hortungs to let him stay until after the party. Somehow it didn't seem very festive to wheel out a corpse."

"For God's sake, Clarence," Lucy hissed through smiling lips. "That is the stupidest thing you've ever done!"

"I know," he said.

"Well, did you at least put the lid down on the casket?"

"Of course! We also tried to mask the coffin with books and the globe, but it doesn't look good."

"Well, lock the library door. For God's sake, Clarence!" Lucy continued to smile and pour.

Dr. Rally turned around and nearly jumped out of his skin. "What the hell is that?" he pointed to the other end of the dining table.

"Well, tonight we're picking the meat off a roasted pig! Doesn't it look wonderful?" Lucy smiled brightly.

By 9:30 the mansion was jumping. Lucy had made several trips into the powder room, each time emerging with a pitcher of Everclear. In an effort to persuade the Hortung twins to stop guarding the library door like a pair of Poe's ravens, she plied them with cups of punch and encouraged them to circulate. Everyone was having fun. She had never heard the faculty laugh and talk so much. Even old Sherman of the Art Department was heehawing hysterically with a math professor and new science teacher in the corner. Unshaven and paunchy, he leaned against the wall and guffawed. His bald head and grizzled beard shone with perspiration. He paid no attention to her as she moved past, for he was absorbed in telling a ribald tale.

Happy Lucy Rally strolled through the crowd, hugging various guests, welcoming them to her home; asking about families and their plans for the holidays. She inquired about Christmas shopping and wished them the merriest of holidays. In the living room she thanked the musicians for their beautiful music and asked them to lead the group in caroling later. In the dining room she thanked Brad for his grand buffet, stressing each dish's magnificent presentation. She thanked the servers, the coat stewards, the kitchen staff, the car valets. She was filled with gratitude. And then she noticed Bitsy Sherman, the infamous art department chair's wife.

Lucy Rally had never cared for Bitsy, a gigantic Viking woman with long golden hair piled on top of her head. Bitsy was much younger than her husband and abnormally buxom. She taught in the nursing department, and Lucy had heard housekeepers whisper about Bitsy's access to various drugs. Bitsy was an unhappy hypochondriac. Anyone innocently greeting Bitsy with "How are you?" was made to regret it. Apparently, she suffered every malady known to womankind, and Lucy made it a policy to avoid her like the wagon of death. Tonight, Bitsy languished on a living room sofa with huge shoeless feet, covered in bandages, propped on the antique coffee table. She was groaning, complaining about her perennially blistered feet, cracked heels, and ingrown toenails. Her voice in the living room was as loud as her husband's in the foyer.

Grant Sherman was schmoozing while his wife was oozing. Lucy headed for the punchbowl. One sip wouldn't hurt.

Then Lucy decided it was time for them to play *Dirty Santa*. Earlier in the evening she had put Clarence's secretary, Cora Greeson, in charge. The totally organized Cora had instructed the partygoers to place their wrapped gifts under the gigantic Christmas tree in the Great Room. Then she had the guests draw a number from a cut-glass bowl. During the evening, Cora had taped tiny numbers to each gift. The person who had number "one" would claim the corresponding gift with a "one" taped to it. Then person "two" could choose between the number "two" gift—still wrapped—or if he wanted the number "one" gift, he could have that one and give the number "one" person the unwrapped number "two" gift. The claiming progressed. It was possible that by the time the numbers had reached "one hundred," the number "one" gift could move ninety-nine times.

Sometimes, the claiming and reclaiming caused people to become antagonistic. Other times it was fun. Fun, for everyone except he who had drawn "one."

Mountainview loved to play Dirty Santa at their parties. But because it was such a rude, selfish, cutthroat game, Lucy had never before allowed it to be played in her home.

They got off to a fine start. The first five people unwrapped their gifts — lovely little Christmas ornaments — and seemed satisfied. But Susan Madigan from the Math Department had drawn the number six, and when she opened her gift the room filled with *ooohs* and *aaahs*. She had unwrapped a tree-topper, a platinum blond angel, with sequined wings, wearing a golden brocade robe. Every woman in the room plotted to take her home at the end of the evening. They elbowed their husbands to fight for her, too.

Susan Madigan was furious when she lost the angel and sat on the floor sulking as the angel was passed from player to player. The more punch they consumed, the more aggressive they became. Finally, John Smith, the librarian, number thirty-eight, unwrapped a crimson and gold nutcracker, which produced the same drama.

The game droned on. Then a glitzy toy soldier, number ninety-one, picked things back up. Guests wandered back and forth from the punchbowl. Lucy's husband's face was a glistening red. She had forgotten to warn him to lay off.

The last person to retrieve a gift was the Viking bandaged nurse, Bitsy Sherman. She pulled herself to her bandaged feet and limped to the tree. Everyone was relieved that the angel, the nutcracker, and the toy soldier were safe. Then she turned to the roomful of people and smiled. She stalled theatrically, teetering. Then she headed across the room.

"I'll just take that friggin' angel."

Sober Annette White, the librarian, was holding the angel. Her face reddened as Bitsy lurched toward her. Annette spoke lowly and evenly, "This angel is safe, and you, Bitsy Sherman, are a terrible bitch."

The room roared.

"More food and drink?" cried Lucy from the wide doorway. "Please come back for more!"

"Did you just call me a bitch?" Bitsy asked Annette.

"It's getting late," said Annette. "I really must go."

People flooded toward the foyer: some headed back into the dining room; others toddled upstairs for coats and scarves; some staggered toward the front door. Lucy dispensed loaves of cranberry bread wrapped in red and gold satinique. Tied to each loaf was a Christmas tree ornament: a pink porcelain pig in a holly wreath with an apple in its mouth.

When her loopy guests opened the front door, they were hit by violent snow and swirling sleet. Finally, the Dean of Students found the student valets watching television in the basement. They refused to go outside, saying the weather was too wild.

"It's horrible out there," Brad agreed.

With many of the others, Lucy returned to the warm dining room. When the doorbell rang and Dr. Rally answered it, an icy blast swept into the dining room. Lucy saw revolving red lights.

"Sorry to disturb you folks," one of two officers said. "But if any of you plan to drive more than a couple of blocks from here, you'd better change your minds. We're in the middle of an ice storm, and the roads are impassable. Better plan to stay where you are until morning."

The crowd panicked. Some rushed outside and drove away regardless, but most were too rattled. None of these was entirely sober. It was obvious they wouldn't make it home.

Lucy felt her organizational skills slipping away. But her husband took control. "I forbid any of you to leave the premises!" He turned to the musicians. "Play something loud and lively. Let's make the best of a bad situation."

The crowd followed Dr. Rally into the Great Room, where he alternately twirled the ladies and dipped and dove with sweeping dance steps. Then he announced, "Call your babysitters, and tell them you won't be home tonight."

Lucy marveled at her husband. Like a flock of inebriated sheep, the faculty followed his instructions. She looked across the room and saw Brad watching her. Slowly and carefully, she made her way to him.

"Brad," she said, "if you tell anybody, I'll kill you."

"Believe me, Mrs. R., I wouldn't tell for a million dollars."

The band tuned up for a bunny hop. Folks lined up and grabbed each other by the waist. Lucy was seized and pushed into the line as everyone kicked to the right, then the left, then hop hop hopped. The entire downstairs throbbed to the music.

Lucy danced and kicked until she thought she'd fall over; then she decided she must have air. Was she having a stroke, a heart attack, maybe a hot flash? She extricated herself and made her way past the wild faculty and staff.

She heard her husband admonishing some of the men: "Hey, guys! No going outside to piss! You're liable to hit a downed live wire on the ground and fry yourselves!"

What remarkable leadership skills! she thought. She needed more punch and headed for the dining room.

Later, still hot and unsteady, Lucy walked the length of the living room, through the French doors, into the garden room and stood, surrounded by windows. The storm had abated, and the moon cast an icy blue glow. The lawn and trees glittered as if covered with diamonds.

"Oh, baby. Ooooh, baby. Yore warmin' up my skillet!"

Lucy froze at the sound of the familiar voice. Slowly she turned. Beyond her prize giant schefflera, four legs protruded from the end of the chaise lounge.

"Oh, baby. Ooooh, baby."

Two of the feet wore familiar-looking dark socks; the other two were wrapped in bandages. Lucy slipped back and ducked into the library. She slid into one of the winged-back chairs beside the fireplace, and breathing deeply, she labored to re-gain her composure.

Bitsy Sherman! That fornicating witch! But who was the man? Not Bitsy's husband. Lucy thought she'd seen him heading downstairs to the game room for a poker party. Still, she believed she'd seen the dark-socked feet before. There was gold stitching on the heels.

She looked around the dimly-lit library. The dying fire cast a gloomy glow, but gradually her eyes focused on Old Tom Lovett's coffin, strewn with books. The walls were still lined with flowers. She rose and felt her way to the double doors. They were locked. "Of course! That's how we kept the faculty out," she reminded herself. She unlocked the doors and opened them. The bunny hoppers bounded down the hall and turned into the library.

The crowd bumped, jumped, and hopped through the library. Lucy managed to turn on a lamp, and someone yelled, "That's Old Tom Lovett in the coffin there! He left the school a lot of money. He's Mountainview's Santa Claus!"

The basketball coach swept the books from casket and opened the lid. "Let's give him a big send-off!"

Lucy remonstrated, "You really mustn't do that," but she was pinned to the wall and her words were lost in the music and shouting. *Where the hell are those Hortung ghouls when you need them?*

The dancers swept through the library, the garden room and the living room, making their way down the hall to the library again. There was no beginning or end. They missed not a right kick, a left kick or a hop hop hop. As they danced past the casket, they patted Old Tom. Some reached in and shook his cold hand. Surely Lucy was having a nightmare.

"Santa looks sad," someone yelled.

"Santa, how thin you are!" Hop hop hop.

"Someone bring him some punch." Hop hop hop.

Lucy broke away. Where was her husband? She ran through to the dining room, where some of the dancers were filling a pitcher with punch for old Tom.

"You must not do that!" she shouted.

"It's a sendoff! Santa is about to take a very long nap!" Amid howls of glee, they headed back to the library, sloshing the lethal liquid. One of the Hortung twins hopped by and panted, "Fabulous party!"

Lucy grabbed him. "Do you realize what's happening to Old Tom Lovett?"

"Frankly, my dear, I don't give a damn," he laughed, then right-kicked away.

Lucy wandered to the foyer and sank to the bottom step of the staircase. *When the trustees hear about this party, the Rallys are history,* but *where in the world is Clarence?*

Suddenly she realized that he was in the garden room

warming Bitsy Sherman's skillet. She had recognized his black socks with gold stitching on the heels.

She pictured him, sock-footed and naked among the thick greenery. Any minute now, the drunken merry-makers would kick too far to the left and discover the amorous couple, and her husband would be exposed to the world. What humiliation! She would never forgive him! Tears streamed down her cheeks and dropped onto her dress, matting the boa.

As Lucy grieved the death of her marriage, the music swelled, and the partygoers' voices grew louder.

"Here comes Santa Claus," hop hop hop.

"Right down Santa Claus lane," hop hop hop.

"Comet and Cupid and all his reindeer," hop hop hop.

Lucy looked up to see the dancers, led by a Hortung twin, kicking and jumping with the accuracy of a drunken chorus line. In the center was the casket, being rolled on its mortuary stand.

Then the other Hortung twin appeared. He shouted to his brother, "It's time to be on our way! I'll get the hearse!"

The crowd danced, hopped and leapt out the door, sliding across the frozen porch and driveway. Sliding this way and that, the fifty or so self-appointed pallbearers loaded the casket. The band played on as the twins climbed into the front seat.

"Thank you for a marvelous evening!" they called, leaning out the windows and waving. The hearse began inching down the curved driveway.

Suddenly, a terrible crash.

The music stopped. All were too stunned to move.

I'm to blame for this disaster, Lucy thought. *I've killed the Hortungs!*

From beyond the curve in the icy driveway, two bent figures appeared. Stumbling, they held on to each other.

"Oh, Mrs. Rally," one of them sing-songed. "May we spend the night? Seems old Santa Claus Tom is wrapped around a tree!"

Clarence stood in the doorway. "What in God's name is going on? What have you people been doing?"

The faculty ignored him as they laughed and relived the near fatal accident, howling over the word *fatal*.

Dr. Rally reached out to Lucy. "Why didn't you send someone to get me?"

"Because you were busy having sex with Bitsy Sherman!" she hissed.

"Woman! Have you lost your mind?"

"Don't speak to me! From now on, you can address my attorney!"

For the rest of the night, most of the faculty ate, drank and played games. Some crawled into beds or made pallets on the hall floor. Still laughing, the Hortungs descended to the basement poker party. With a chenille afghan and a soft pillow, Lucy made herself a bed on the leather sofa and lay down in the library.

She was getting her comeuppance. But why? And for what? All she had wanted was for the faculty to love her. She hadn't intended to bring them to their knees, stranded in an ice storm. She hadn't meant for her punch to nearly kill the Hortungs. And the worst part — the lethal punch had caused her husband to unleash a passion for the bandaged Brunhilde!

Lucy lay awake. Gradually she shifted from guilt to practicality. She concentrated on the stranded faculty, wondered if they were warm enough in their makeshift beds; wondered if she had something to feed them for breakfast. Maybe she and Brad could scare up enough cheese and eggs for a roast pork and egg casserole. Thank goodness for the pig! She left her cozy make-shift bed, grabbed pencil and paper, and created a recipe.

With the student workers' help, Lucy and Brad prepared enough food to feed the faculty and staff a light breakfast. The highway department had begun sanding the streets so the Rallys' guests left before noon.

Grant Sherman came to the kitchen to say good-bye. "I want to thank you for your hospitality," he said with a grin. "We appreciate everything you've done for us. It was a most extraordinary night."

Wearing her bedraggled red dress and a pair of white flip-flops, Lucy walked with Grant to the front door. Surprised that he acted so happy, she asked, "Who won the poker game?"

"I don't know," he answered. "I didn't play poker. You'll have to ask your husband. Thank you again, Mrs. Rally. Have a very merry Christmas and a wonderful New Year."

Bitsy waited beside the front door, clutching her Barbie angel. "Thanks, Mrs. R.," she said. The bandages were unraveled.

President and Mrs. Rally stood on the porch and waved good-bye to their guests. A ragtag army of educators, staff, and students called out, "Merry Christmas! We'll see you next year!"

POETRY

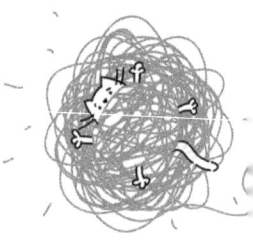

SUMMERTIME GIRLS, 1960

That summer I wore a black and white highly inflatable
   swimsuit—
gorgeous, Mother said, with my silky Coppertone tan.

A season for sundresses, boys and fast driving,
when Elvis caused jitterbug fever
at night, Little Richard, the dirty bop.
And on hot afternoons, by the Country Club pool,
our mothers taught us to play bridge.

Flattened by the yellow West Texas sky
we waited for boyfriends to finish their eighteen.
Sipping pink lemonade, we practiced our smoking skills
and trumped each other's tricks.

My father's young caddy stood at the edge,
watching children splash at the shallow end
his fingers—baby blacksnakes—
curled in the chain link wire.
Dusty and hot he sagged on the fence
wearing long sleeved shirt, khaki pants, someone else's
   shoes.

We finished our bridge game, then walked past him, oblivious of the future.

Like bright, glistening pennies, we threw ourselves off the high diving board. And while the black boy watched, we plunged deep deep deep into cool wet blue.

ABSTRACT ART

Across the wide canvas
a broad horizontal band
of azure blue.
Another color below –
a thick stripe of spun-wheat gold.
And at the bottom a stretch
of rich clay red.
"Abstract art at its finest!"
jurors exclaim.
"Is it a Jackson Pollock?"
Au contraire,
it's an Oklahoma summer landscape.

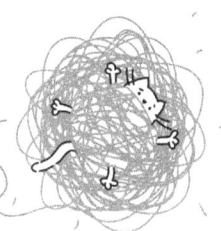

THE CRITIC

Orange hair in spikes,
raccoon make-up,
pierced eyebrows, neck rose tattoo,
short chartreuse dress, black hose.
She stood at my book signing
in pointy four- inch heels.
Said she could write a story better than mine
if only she had better luck,
but she keeps her laptop on her cook stove
and can't stand up long enough
to write anything.
Besides, after her hysterectomy,
she's forgotten how to spell.

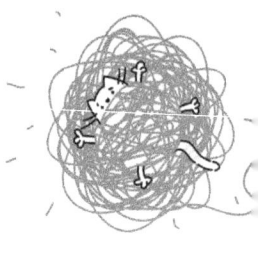

THE SUMMER OF OUR DISCONTENT

The heat rises and the wind blows.
I hibernate like a bear under the air-conditioner.
The news from Zambia, deepest, darkest Africa,
Where my daughter studies AIDS,
And her daughters study lions, giraffes, and elephants
On safaris, is that it's cool.
Really cool, Grandmother, in every possible way.
(Not fraught with peril but cool.)

I went to the wedding of my best friend's daughter
Where the fat preacher wore a plaid suit,
And the groom wore glitzy pink socks.
Clutching the altar, the bride lip-synched, "Wind Beneath my Wings"
While the groom rocked, heel to toe, threatening to topple.
At the reception the bride and groom entertained us—
Sang, danced, and slugged down shots called "Blue Panties."
Then skyrocketed away in a black Lamborghini
Rented over the internet.
We guests lined the hot driveway, waving sparklers,
Fearing our hair would catch fire.

The Oklahoma wind blows, no rain in the forecast, and fires rage.
But in Zambia it is winter, and it is wet and cool, Grandmother,
Really cool.

X

X belongs to Xs and Os,
Xanadu, X chromosomes, Xerox, X-ratings and X-rays.
He's a masculine figure, as in xenogamy, or the Greek ancestor, Xuthus.
A wooden figure, xylophone,
landscape figure, green, xeriscape,
or surgical figure, xyster, scraping bones.

X sometimes travels alone, almost a xenophobe, resentful when used
nonchalantly, as in Xmas, or by persons unable to write their own names.
His sisters, K and Q, accomplish more, in kindness and queenliness,
but X really doesn't mind. He's a practical old letter,
and while K kindles and Q quakes, X works behind the scenes—
extinguishes, examines, extricates, explains,
and exterminates only under duress.

Occupying just one and a third page in *The American
  Heritage Dictionary*,
X could have an inferiority complex,
because his rival, Z, occupies four.
Then he remembers the historical X-shaped cross
 the apostle Peter chose for crucifixion.
Despite his shyness, X smiles at extravaganza.

X works but cannot accomplish everything.
In war? No exit.
Hurricanes? earthquakes? Extinction.

OCTOBER HAYSTACKS

Riding home in the back seat
a child on each side of me
we count the autumn trees —
orange, crimson, gold.

We pass flat yellow meadows,
and giant round bales of hay,
like wandering tan elephants,
strolling to a carnival.

Now we begin to play our heartbreak.
Years stretch ahead, a pasture of Octobers.
I see my life now, a pattern,
the years, like rows of Monet's haystacks.
But drab, the light shining wrongly.
Without you, riding home.

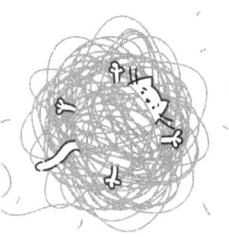

THE FUNERAL OF A FIRST HUSBAND

What do you do about your first husband's funeral?
if you were his second wife
and three more followed
along with no-telling-how-many girlfriends?
Do you wear black or another solemn color and waltz in with a flair?
Do you send flowers or a card to the widow?
commiserating? congratulating?
For advice with this social conundrum, whom do you ask?
Miss Manners? *Dear Abby*? *Dear Ann*?
Erma Bombeck would have made a wry comment.
Alas, she's not commenting anymore.
If all the ex-wives and girlfriends attended the service as a herd,
you could sit together and raise a loud lamentation
about what a sorry son-of-a-bitch he was.
But that would embarrass the children and grandchildren
and one great, on the way,
now a sizeable bump beneath your granddaughter's green jacket
sitting at the front of the church with the rest of the family.
Yours and his.

So out of love for the treasured bump,
you, along with your second husband,
teeth clenched; both go to your first husband's funeral.
And you might even manage to cry. A little.

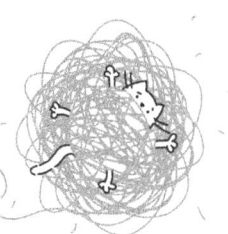

SARAH PEARL HAMMOND

When we were growing up
our greatest fear was a plague of elephantiasis
leaving us looking like
Sarah Pearl Hammond,
 six-foot tall, big-boned black
who came to town every Saturday
from somewhere down in the bottoms.
Her legs were like walking cypress trunks.

Thirty eager white Rainbow girls,
selling at a bake sale, raising dough for Charity
spelled with a capital C,
always watched Her Blackship
lumbering through the grocery
swinging heavy, swollen flesh,
head wrapped in starched white turban,
huge silver hoops in her earlobes,
gathered cotton print skirt,
moccasin boats,
buying rice and beans.

Our biology teacher, Mrs. Bittle,
while presenting a lesson on insects,
said that if one of us perchance were bitten
by an ambitious mosquito
that also had sucked on old Pearl,
flown clear from "the dark stinking flats,"
into one of our "pleasant white houses,"
perhaps drawn by a light in the window,
we also would catch the disease.

From then on, the challenge of youth
was avoiding all mosquitoes.

And then Pearl died.
"Self-inflicted gunshot wound,"
the coroner said.
Our town went silent – but for only a moment.
Then we swept guilt under our doormats,
and we Rainbow girls carried on.

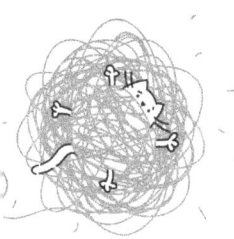

THE ELEPHANT AND THE CAT

An elephant sits upon my chest.
After the *please don't let me die* prayer,
after ten hours of gloved hands whittling,
the creature has come to rest.
Immaculately wrapped in white gauze and tape,
he takes up all the space.
I cannot see his eyes.
"How long will I have the elephant?" – the question,
"He will gradually disappear." – the answer.
"I have nothing at home to feed him."

I was warned to expect a Mack truck,
not a heavy beast.
"You are very lucky. He
only comes to special people."
Nurses giggle in the hall.

The pachyderm goes home with me.
Traveling in a wheelchair,
I carry him on my breastbone.
Throughout the ride he doesn't move,
and I do not feel special.

He doesn't lose an ounce,
but smashes, crushes and
grinds me into the sheets
until I become a thin film of pain
melting into the mattress.

The cat jumps onto my bed.
Sniffing, he tiptoes onto my chest,
and the heaviness increases.
Ears back, nose down, flicking tail, soft growls.
Disapproving of the elephant, he hisses.
He looks me in the eye and moans,
"Is this what you've become?"
Leaping down, he runs away.

They bring me soup and crackers.
They bring me cookies and ice cream.
They do not bring my cat.

But late at night in murky darkness
 — the great beast must be sleeping —
I feel a plop on the side of the bed
and tiny footsteps toward me.
With stealth, the cat creeps to my head.
He licks my face, kisses my eyelids, sips my tears.
Sharing my pillow, he stretches to touch my neck, my
    shoulders.
With clawless paws he massages,
purring at motorboat throttle,
now kneading, kneading bread.

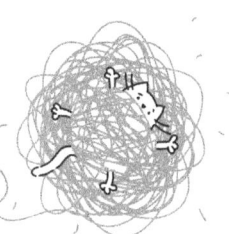

THE WHEELER CEMETERY

Flat as a baseball field,
and named for a Confederate general,
in the middle of the Texas Panhandle
the Wheeler County Cemetery stretches
with iron gates open and welcomes all.

And there my people lie.
Pioneers in this grassless, windswept place,
their headstones lined up like choirboys.

We go back generations.
One grandmother buried next to five babies;
her husband beside his second wife.
Their gravestones remind us
how quickly we can be replaced.

The wind blows, but the stones stand steady.
Stubborn, they won't be broken by West Texas storms.
Here calligraphy and etchings really matter.
My parents' names survived a tornado.

But those cremated have flat marble slabs
over metal urns buried deep in sandy soil.
My sister, between two husbands,
their lonely plaques as desperate as a dust storm.
All adult plots are equal in size.
The babies, smaller, but the same.
A tribute to democracy.
As if Death really cares.

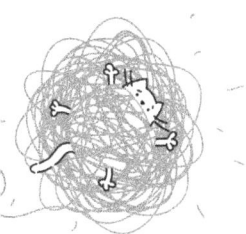

GRIEF

Against a gray September sky, a gander plummets.
Fifty in formation whoosh a turn, descend and land.
Solemnly they encircle the dead,
web-footed mourners in a funeral march.
Then, synchronized, they float-walk to nearby berm
and wait, as one lone goose remains behind with him.
She stiffens, stretches, prods.
The people on my terrace, hushed,
watch her turn and waddle to the others.
The geese are still and mute as statues.
Suddenly, as if obeying a sergeant's whistle,
already in their lines they rise,
a grey-green-blue-black mass, wing south,
 honk in concert and disappear.
"They mate for life," Jack says,
and goes to find a shovel.

QUANDRY

Tomorrow my husband leaves for his octogenarians' golf-
    ing trip
and I have only one concern —
what if our ancient cat dies while he's gone?
Seventeen human years equal 105 cat years.
He's older than I by three decades,
so surely, I'll survive him.

Who can I find to dig his grave?
On the golf course outside our bedroom window
next to the graves of three other cats
against all Country Club rules.
They made us take the crosses down.

I'll tack up a sign on the bulletin board —
"Who will help me bury my cat?"
I'll need a hole twenty inches wide and a foot deep.
I'll remove his collar, wrap him in a soft towel
and on my knees, lower him into the ground.
Then pray, "Now I lay me down to sleep..."
Hoping like hell no one yells, "Fore!"

Later, after the grave digger has gone,
I'll be overcome by brutal anguish, heartsick tears,
and most of all, the missing, the wretched missing
one so marvelously and completely loved.

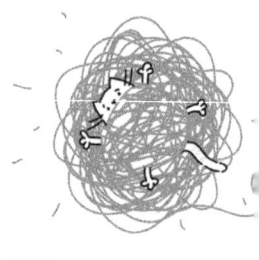

AS WE BECOME OUR MOTHERS

At seventy, most of us have learned
the birthday surprise
by looking in the mirror
or hearing our own voices.
All horrors present and accounted for:
we have become the women who,
as flitting girls,
jittery as birds,
we complained about.
Our mothers.

We remember brooding staircases,
celery-colored carpets
and kitchen floors that gleamed
hard and smooth as ice.
Fairy tales and nightly prayers
gave way to dire warnings of
things we must not dare to do,
but we did anyway – or wished we had.

Regal, red-lipped, they take off hats and gloves,
fold eyeglasses, smile and nod,
knowing, across the years,
what we know now, at seventy.
As we become our mothers
and our daughters become us.

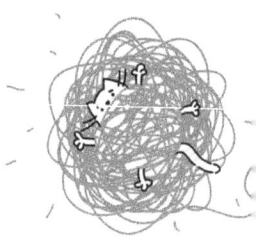

THE BLACK MADONNAS

Art historians say there are between four hundred and five hundred
Black Madonna statues and paintings scattered throughout Europe.
People believe they are endowed with supernatural powers
and pray to them earnestly, fervently.
I have seen four in Europe, one in Africa.

In Poland, the shrine of Jasna Gora, where the
painted mother and child are elegantly decorated
according to the seasons of the church.

The second, a statue in the monastery of Montserrat.
High in the Spanish mountains, overwhelmed by
chanting monks and deafening organ music,
I knelt and touched the black Christ Child's knee.

The third, a painting in Paris at Chartres Cathedral,
with Byzantine infant holding a Bible.
Both mother and baby stiffly raised huge hands to greet me.

Next, a large statue on a busy street in Prague, kept in a cage
protruding from the corner of the House of the Black
Madonna.
Riding a tour bus, I passed by her each day.

The last, in a cathedral in Dakar, Senegal,
the tall, slender black Lady of Deliverance
held her ebony Christ child in her left arm,
both wearing long white glittering triangular robes.

I have known a real-life black Madonna —
the housekeeper of my childhood, in the fields of Oklahoma,
rescued a Cherokee newborn from his mother
who held a shovel, about to bash in his head.

Our Anna Mae took him home, made him hers,
and named him Bobby Lee,
while the rest of us called him the Miracle Baby,
saved by the grace of God.

ESSAYS

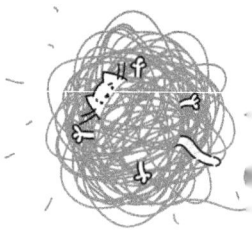

CHRISTMAS EVE IN SENEGAL

*"This is what the Lord says—
the Redeemer and Holy One of Israel—
to him who was despised and abhorred by the nation,
to the servant and rulers:
'Kings will see you and rise up,
princes will see and bow down,
because of the Lord, who is faithful,
the Holy One of Israel, who has chosen you.'"*
Isaiah 49:7

The angel onstage wore a shiny, long blue dress. Black, tall, and statuesque, she was a girl of twelve or thirteen, and she faced the congregation, her wings glittering. She turned and spoke to another teenager onstage, a girl playing Elizabeth.

"You will give birth to a child!" the angel announced in French. "This child will grow to be a great leader. And he will prepare the world for the Messiah."

The angel moved across the stage, where a girl portraying Mary stood. "You will bear *that* child," the angel proclaimed. "He is the Messiah, the Son of God, the Holy

One of Israel, the Prince of Peace."

Thus, the Christmas pageant began. Our family was visiting an Evangelical church in Dakar, Senegal, West Africa, where our daughter served in the Peace Corps. It was Christmas Eve.

Like a medieval morality play, the drama unfolded loosely, rambunctiously, with great creativity and unexpected humor. The actors were all children. Brilliantly dressed, they delivered their lines with strong voices and robust theatrical gestures.

The entire production emphasized not only the traditional spiritual message of the Christmas story, but also the humanness of us all. When the smallest angel announced the birth of the baby Jesus to the shepherds, she forgot her lines. The oldest angel—the willowy one—irritably thumped the smaller child's wings and delivered the announcement herself.

Later in the production, three elegant wise men haughtily strode into the castle of King Herod—and Queen Herod. When Herod heard the wise men's questions regarding the whereabouts of the new king, he bristled, "*Where* is the King of the Jews?" And then he boasted, "*I* am the King of the Jews!"

His wife, hands on hips, stomped her foot and shouted, "And *I* am the Queen of the Jews!" The crowd roared with laughter.

The pageant did not end with the adoration of the Christ child in the manger. That traditional scene was followed by a return to the inn, where Mary and Joseph had been turned away. In this final scene, the innkeeper, a Wolof tribal boy of about ten, bitterly wept, threw a broom, tore his cleaning rags, and banged his head upon a table, when he realized his mistake.

The innkeeper's haunting portrayal reminded the audience that Christ is always in our midst, and that we may foolishly ignore Him or turn Him away.

After several curtain calls, the performance ended. And then we sang. A musician from the States—an elderly white woman—pounded an old upright piano, playing familiar hymns for the crowd of several hundred Europeans, Africans, and Americans.

Led by the Senegalese choir director, we held hands and swayed to piano and drumbeat, singing simultaneously in English, German, and French, along with the tribal languages of Wolof and Seder: "Silent Night," "Hark the Herald Angels Sing," "Joy to the World."

That Christmas Eve, our family participated in an event that highlighted human creativity, celebrated the diversity of God's people, proclaimed the glory of Christ, and affirmed God's love for His world. We experienced Christian worship on a level we had never before known.

ALL LAID OUT

When I'm all laid out and candle-lit, I want to wear something snazzy. Something that will cause the mourners to gasp and then smile and say, "That old girl sure knew how to dress!"

If it's wintertime, please bury me in my Christmas red wool suit, my faux pearl necklace, with my shoulders wrapped in a red cashmere shawl. If it's summer, put me in my fuchsia silk party dress and crystal earrings, an outfit I generally reserve for weddings. If it's autumn, let me wear the aqua suede get-up, along with my turquoise jewelry. And if it's spring, put me in the little pink number with the short swishy skirt that looks sassy when I dance.

If by some twist of fate, I live to be a hundred, I really want to go out in outrageous style: my black velvet millennium formal (with the extremely high slit up the side), along with my rhinestone tiara and black feather boa.

Our African American sisters know how to dress right for important occasions. Read the book entitled *Crowns* or see the musical by the same name. The book is full of pictures of beautiful black women wearing magnificent hats. These women wear their very best clothes and gorgeous hats each time they enter the House of the Lord. If you're not willing to dress up on Sundays when you go to visit God, they reason, then what on earth *are* you willing to dress up for? What occasion could ever be more important than a worship service? As far as I'm concerned, these ladies have a very strong argument. Alleluia, Sister, and Amen!

Being Dead is No Excuse: The Official Southern Ladies' Guide to Hosting the Perfect Funeral is a cookbook that stresses the socially accepted, prim and proper way to have a really swell farewell-to-life celebration. Polished silver and all.

I agree with Gayden Metcalfe, the author of this clever book, but I'll carry the idea one step further. Being dead is no excuse for wearing tacky grave-clothes.

My Living Will has an addendum, which states, "Let me wear something pretty, comfortable, and warm for all eternity. No pale, flimsy nightgown and robe set and above all, NO JEANS."

As far as I'm concerned, jeans look good on everybody else but me. Almost everywhere I go, 95% of the women are wearing them. Oprah and practically every other celebrity have glamorized them, but I've never even found a pair that fits.

I'm like the comic strip character Cathy, whose worst nightmare is a dressing room full of jeans. Honestly, to me, looking into a dressing room mirror and trying on a pair of jeans is the ultimate slap in the face with a wet squirrel.

If you come to my funeral and I'm wearing jeans, it means one thing: whoever dressed me up thinks I'm not going on to The Good Place. Or perhaps that person carries an abnormally huge grudge against me and wants to punish me forever.

Imagine that.

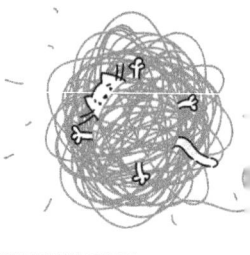

LONG LIVE THE SWEET POTATO QUEENS

St. Patrick's Day has come and gone, and so has the Sweet Potato Queen Parade in Jackson, Mississippi. The Sweet Potato Queens Club was started in the early 1980's by the royal ringleader Jill Conner Browne, who talked the mayor of Jackson into letting a bunch of sassy, outrageous women ride on a float in the annual St. Paddy's Day Parade. By now, The Sweet Potato Queens have taken over the whole shootin' match, and people come from all over the world to see them.

First of all, the Sweet Potato Queens are women with an agenda. They stand for something. Mainly, they represent all those millions of Southern Women who never won a beauty contest or were never crowned Queen of Something. Yes, it's hard to believe, but it's true that there are millions of lovely women in this category. Most of these current Queens have never even entered a beauty contest. But they put on their infamous costumes and impress everybody with their deliciously wicked, fun-loving ways.

When the Sweet Potato Queens dress up, they all wear identical uniforms: a huge red wig (Remember the old Southern adage – "The higher the hair, the closer to God"); a short bright green sequined dress which barely covers the fanny (with humongous hips and boobs built in); white high-heeled boots; white over-the-elbow fringed gloves; huge pointed sunglasses; and a rhinestone tiara.

In their speech and behavior, the Sweet Potato Queens are more than a little naughty. You might even call them wild. They like men, they like all the stuff their men buy for them, they like to cook and to eat what they've cooked, and they especially like their pals, the other Sweet Potato Queens. Sometimes, the things they say and do would make even that rich little witch Scarlett O'Hara blush. For example, their frank discussion of Fat Mama's Knock You Naked Margaritas.

The Sweet Potato Queens may be unlucky in beauty pageants, but they're lucky in love. They know how to handle men, sometimes juggling several boyfriends at a time. The married Queens are true to their husbands, and they have many tricky ways to keep their guys in line. If every American woman could manage her husband like a true Queen, there'd be no need for the "Dr. Phil Show."

By now the Sweet Potato Queens have become an international group of women. In fact, there are over 7,000 members of the SPQ Club. They're pert, perky and proud of it.

I wanna be a Sweet Potato Queen. But not really.

Tromping down the middle of the street, wearing a heavy wig and a tight big-boobed dress could seriously increase a woman's hot flashes. Think about it. The original eight Queens (Brown plus seven others) must be middle-aged by now. And they're the only ones allowed to ride on a float in the parade. All the others are considered Sweet Potato Queen Wannabes. One of these St. Paddy's Days, some of those hot menopausal women might just ignite out on the pavement, creating a serious scene of spontaneous combustion.

Being a latecomer to the group, I'd have to stomp around in those boots and boobs, along with a cast of thousands. Not me. I want to ride.

So maybe I'll start my own group. Not red hats, not purple dresses, not sweet Adelaides, not clogging dancers, and not marching lesbians.

I wanna be an Artichoke Empress. My outfit will be soft, lightweight, and flowing, sorta like a nightgown. And my crown will be shaped like an artichoke. Everything a soft vegetable green, I'll put the glam in glamour.

I've chosen the artichoke because the only cooking advice my mother ever gave me was, "Honey, almost any dish can be improved by the flavor of an artichoke." So, I'm using the artichoke as a symbol of improvement.

So why not an international group of aging, nightgown-wearing Artichoke Empresses? Lounging about, propped up by cushions, riding in the back of a flatbed truck? That ought to add sizzle to any parade!

We'll have a few rules to keep order in the ranks, but

our major interest will be eating, drinking, wearing, and saying what we darned well please. Same as the SPQ's.

As the Sweet Potato Queens age, they'll develop varicose veins, fallen arches, poochy stomachs and sagging breasts, and they'll get tired of stomping around in their smothering outfits and painful boots. When that happens, we'll welcome them into our group of Artichoke Empresses.

And we'll all ride in the parade.

By the way, girls, "*The Sweet Potato Queens' Book of Love*" should be on your reading list. And "*The Sweet Potato Queens' Fat-Ass Cookbook (and Financial Planner)*" should be on your recipe shelf.

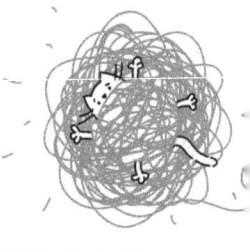

THE GRAND PASSION OF DESPERATE HOUSECATS

Samson and Lila are lovers.
Oh, how those two cats can love.

Recently my neighbor, Wendy, telephoned in a panic and asked if I was aware that the City Council has passed an ordinance forbidding pet cats to roam at large. If you live within city limits, your cat must either stay on your property or else be leashed, which is ridiculous.

"Can you imagine?" Wendy screamed. "This law goes against nature! It'll kill Samson, since he's definitely an *outside* cat! I can't keep him happy *indoors*!"

"And it'll kill my cat, Lila, or else *I'll* kill her, because she'll ruin my drapes, carpets, and furniture," I answered. "If she destroys my house, I'm sending the City Council the bill."

"Whatever were those lawmakers thinking? You can't teach a cat to heel, and you can't force an outdoor cat to live inside. They're not dogs, for goodness sake!" Wendy lamented.

Wendy's and my cats were destined for each other. A huge, furry gray hulk, Samson hankers after petite yellow fuzzy Lila, and the way they carry on in public is outrageous. Even after two litters of kittens, which resulted in neutering and spaying, these two star-crossed lovers are hot for each other. Hunka hunka, honey. They're in love — they're all shook up!

They have no intention of becoming mealy-mouthed housecats. Indoors, they spew, spray, scratch, hiss, throw up fur-balls, and meow miserably.

Before the infamous City Council ruling, Samson visited Lila in our front yard twice a day, for mutual face licks, scampering and sun baths. As they cavorted with feline glee, I watched them with envy.

One morning I told my husband, "I don't think you love me as much as Samson loves Lila."

"Listen, honey, just because I don't chase you across the driveway and over a fence, then tackle you and gnaw on your neck, doesn't mean I don't love you. Of course, if you'd prefer rough-house passion, I'm willing to try it," he answered, grinning like the Cheshire cat in *Alice in Wonderland*.

"On second thought," I answered, "please forget I ever mentioned Samson and Lila's torrid love affair."

If love and passion are so strong in these two felines, no wonder the whole world practically revolves around those emotions. From stories in the Bible to episodes on modern soap operas we get love and lust aplenty. We find slews of examples of historical and fictional characters overcome by Steam Heat:

> *David and Bathsheba*
> *Marc Anthony and Cleopatra*
> *Romeo and Juliet*
> *Napoleon and Josephine*
> *Rhett and Scarlett*
> *Bogey and Bacall*
> *Johnny Cash and June Carter*
> *Brad and Jennifer*
> Oops! Omit that final one.

Well, maybe Grand Passion doesn't *always* last forever. Perhaps we shouldn't expect it to. And certainly, we shouldn't take our cues from the animal kingdom, as far our behavior is concerned. Maybe one reason the divorce rate is so high is that sometimes we act a little like a passel of cats, irresponsible, and not exactly true to our partners or our offspring.

Lawsy mercy, for Grand Passion we certainly shouldn't look to movie and television stars, either. Many celebrities pretend to be smitten with each other, and then turn around and treat one another absolutely rotten.

Instead, perhaps we should look to those few human couples who've put up with each other for fifty years or more and have survived to tell the tale. No doubt we'd learn something about everlasting, passionate love if we listened to their stories of staying together despite unrealized dreams, lost jobs, financial disasters, unplanned pregnancies, rebellious children, rifts with in-laws, problems with elderly parents, and poor health in their own twilight years.

Along with those unsettling stories, there are always stories of loyalty, duty, humor, and devotion. Look at the example of Betty and Gerald Ford, together for over fifty-eight years.

I read somewhere that the institution of marriage is what holds two people together when Grand Passion fails, until they can start loving each other again.

There just might be some truth to that statement.

For Valentine's Day, my husband has promised not to chase me around the block, knock me down, or bite my neck. Instead, we may simply exchange mushy cards, then put on our jammies, scrunch our feet into fuzzy house-slippers, build a blaze in the fireplace, open a bottle of wine and watch a DVD.

That comfortable kind of housecat passion can be mighty grand.

On the other hand, if I live up to my potential, maybe he'll give me that lovely gold necklace I've been hinting for. Maybe we'll get all gussied up and go out for dinner and dancing. Steppin' out with my baby is even passionately grander.

Also, in honor of romance in the animal kingdom, we'll let Samson and Lila have a sleepover in our garage. Neck-biting all night long.

So, in the name of Grand Passion, Happy Valentine's Day to you, one and all.

And Girls, remember – always be *particular*. Or *peculiar*. Whichever is more interesting – to you and the man you love.

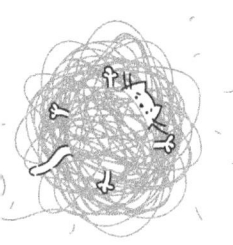

ARE MEN NECESSARY?

I've just read "*Are Men Necessary?*" by Maureen Dowd. This book is a hoot, and I highly recommend it. To women only. Honestly, girls, Maureen knows some stuff we all need to know. But maybe our men folks don't. After all, our men folks give us enough trouble, without getting all riled up about Maureen Dowd's reports on the pitiful nature of the Masculine Gender.

Although the book is entertaining, I was disappointed, because the assertive Maureen, who is a smarty-pants Pulitzer prize-winning columnist for "*The New York Times*," never answers her own question, "Are Men Necessary?"

She could've said, "Yes, they're necessary because they supply an essential ingredient in the Reproductive Act."

Or, she could've said, "No, men aren't necessary because we women can do any job as well as they can, and usually even better."

But the witty Ms. Dowd doesn't give a definitive answer. However, she does tell us about the scientific theory of the Extinction of Man. In the future (a million years from now) there will be no more men. They'll have evolved themselves clean out of existence.

In other words, they're going to become so useless Mother Nature can't stand to have them around anymore.

Here's the theory: The Y (male) chromosome has been shedding genes for eons and now is only a fraction of the size of the X (female) chromosome. The Y chromosome is "a mere remnant of its once mighty structure," writes British geneticist Steve Jones. "Men are wilting away. From sperm count to social status and from fertilization to death, as civilization advances, those who bear Y chromosomes are in relative decline." (Hmm. Wonder if that's why there are more women in college now than men?)

As the Y gets weaker, the X gets stronger. Finally, the Y will disappear entirely, leaving only women to run things. So, men will disappear, taking swimsuit editions of *Sports Illustrated* and raised toilet seats with them.

In fact, the X will be so powerful there won't be any need for sexual reproduction as we know it. Little girls will just sprout out of big girls, sort of like the aloe plant in my kitchen.

Well, good grief and shoot the preacher.

Now I'll bet some modern guys might wonder if they have any purpose at all. After all, we women don't even expect them to go out and shoot bears for us anymore. If a bear needs to be shot, we'll shoot it. So, these days we've pretty well-established women as hunters as well as gatherers. Look at the military, if you please.

Listen, I'd rather be drawn and quartered than go back to the old days, when women were property and treated like pea-brains. But if Maureen is right, and men are on their way out, I think this news is pretty alarming for our sisters on down the road. Because women really like men. We like them a lot.

You know, a woman's girlfriends are a lot like cats – smart, pretty, fashion- conscious (all that kitty grooming!), judgmental, interesting, a little wicked, mysterious, and fun. Unfortunately, a cat will leave you if you don't live up to her expectations. Fickleness is definitely a feline trait. So, a gal can never have too many cats, because they wander off, just as she can never have quite enough women friends, because they may up and leave her in the soup.

Men, on the other hand, sit back, veg out, act friendly, and let things happen in their relationships without too much stress, worry or work. They're not as interestingly mysterious as women, but they're not as judgmental, either. Men are a lot like dogs. And the older they get, the doggier they get. In fact, some men are just big old dogs with furniture.

A life-timer husband, one who's in it for the entire marriage trip, is like an old hound dog. He may gobble his food, scratch his stomach, track mud into the house, and ignore your commands, but he's a warm friendly body who bounces with pleasure if you throw him even the smallest bone.

Back to Maureen Dowd's question, "Are Men Necessary?" As far as I'm concerned, men are necessary.

I'd gladly go before the Evolutionary Supreme Court and argue for Mother Nature to let them stay. Specifically, we X chromosomers need the Y's for three main reasons:

1. To fix things. Give a man a power tool and a roll of duct tape, and Whoa, Mama! He gets as busy as old King Kong.

2. To lift and carry. From hoisting heavy upright pianos to transporting sleeping children. Honestly, watching a hunka munka man hold a tiny baby next to his chest will make your gizzard quiver.

3. To cheer us up when we're blue. As in, "Honey, I'm sorry your canary died. Would you stop crying if I bought you a new car?"

When a sensitive hound dog man says that, a woman becomes as happy as a squirrel with a nut in winter, flicking its tail to the rhythm of "Jingle Bells."

I've never understood why Elvis Presley sang *You Ain't Nothin but a Hound Dog* so disparagingly. I like the song but don't agree with the message, which treats hound dogs as low-class, lazy, complaining bums. And poor hunters, to boot.

I'm afraid lover boy Elvis really didn't have a clue about what makes a woman happy. Because one good and faithful lifelong hound dog man is all any smart woman wants or needs.

Are Men Necessary? Poor Maureen Dowd. If she'd ever had the kind of hound dog man I'm talking about, she wouldn't have to ask.

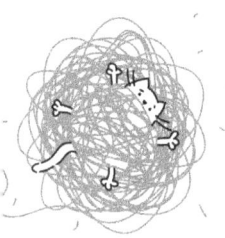

NOT EVEN IN A HANDBASKET

For almost as long as I can remember, I've been headed straight to hell. By people with authority I've been told, "Do not dawdle; do not collect $200.00; do not pass *Go*. Just pick up your crummy little soul and land there."

It started with my mother. When I was six years old and swatted my three-year-old sister for pulling my doll's head off, I called my sister a *fool*. Mother yanked me up by the arm and hissed, "It says in the Bible that he who calls his brother a *fool* will go to hell! Don't you know that?"

Well, no, I didn't know that. From that moment on, I hoped God would take into consideration that I had left my *brother* completely out of my tirade. It was only my *sister* that I'd called a *fool*. And just one time.

"Please, Lord," I tacked onto my nightly prayers. "Don't send me to hell. I called her a *fool* only once, and I didn't mean it!"

Next it was the Baptists. I grew up in a small Texas town evenly divided into Southern Baptists, Church of Christ members, and Methodists. We were Methodists, and mighty proud of it. The Church of Christers claimed that since they allowed no musical instruments in their church services, *they* were the only people in the whole wide world who were in God's good graces, and they were therefore headed for heaven. The Baptists claimed that *they* were the only ones on the right track, since the rest of the townspeople (mainly the Methodists) danced, drank liquor, and went to the movies on Sunday. The Methodists didn't talk too much about heaven and hell, except when threatening their children.

When I was nine, I went to Baptist Bible School with my best friend, Becky Sue Riley. On the last day, the teachers herded us, a whole passel of children, into the church sanctuary, which had a huge stained-glass window showing Jesus holding a sweet-faced lamb, right above the baptismal pool. The preacher stood next to that window, and his message was simple: "Children," he shouted, "Renounce your sins, and *promise never, ever to drink a single drop of liquor!*"

The Bible School teachers stood at the end of each pew and handed out pencils and paper. We kids were instructed to write our tee-totaling promises on the slips of paper, sign our names, and then take the papers down to the front of the sanctuary and place them in a basket on the altar. Right in front of the stained-glass Jesus.

I thought about my grandfather's nightly ritual of pouring a splash of Mogen David wine into a juice glass for my grandmother. He did this to help her get to sleep. Somehow, I couldn't see my grandparents as doomed sinners. My stomach felt as though I'd swallowed an egg as I decided that *never* is a very long time. So, I was the only child in Bible School who did *not* make the Pledge. Automatically, I was headed for hell. It was just a matter of when, not where.

It's been quite worrisome.

And as I age, it gets more and more worrisome. As I listen to my evangelical friends, I realize that, scientifically and genetically speaking, my faith-in-the-fury-of God gene is recessive. I simply cannot get worked up about the rules and regulations regarding humanity's eternal life, *i.e.*, the Spiritual Social Security Plan.

But through the years I've learned to cope, more or less, and have found immense relief in the Presbyterian Church. 'The Frozen Chosen," some call it, because Presbyterians usually choose a scholarly approach rather than an emotional one. Presbyterians historically love research, history, translation, study, and debate, and when there is a conflict in opinions, we pretty well "agree to disagree agreeably."

But now what-do-you-know! Lo and behold, the Evangelicals and the Born-Againers have invaded good ol' staunch, dull Presbyterianism. Again, I've been made to feel that I'm in trouble with the Lord. Once again, on the Day of Judgment, I'll be a goner.

The reasons I'm about to be thrown into the fiery furnace are these:

1. I neither hate nor fear gay people, and I would welcome any of my gay friends as a leader in my church.

2. I believe that God is not exclusive, but inclusive. Religions other than Christianity are not worthless. It's possible that God speaks to different cultures in different ways.

3. I think that to interpret every word, jot and tittle in the Bible literally is not what God intended and a dreadful waste of time.

Now I ask you, who wants to believe that God's a gruff old meanie in the sky, just waiting for somebody to mess up? Certainly not I.

But my Christian Fundamentalist friends believe I'm in grave trouble. As far as they are concerned, my soul is headed straight to hell. How tiresome.

To those well-meaning Crusaders I can only incriminate myself when I answer: blame my Eternal Punishment Gene Deficiency for my very strong, apparently unpopular belief that God is Love.

And because that particular belief overwhelms me so completely, I suppose I'm destined to meet the devil in the hot place.

I will not collect $200.00; I will not pass *Go*. I'll just pick up my sad little soul and land there.

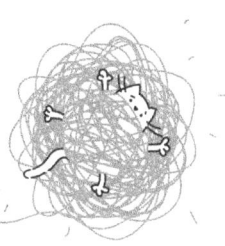

A SKUNK BY ANY OTHER NAME WOULD SMELL AS SWEET

Just when I think life has reached ultimate weirdness, it gets a little weirder.

Recently I met a woman who has a pet skunk. This lady and I were both patients at a physical therapy clinic. We both had back injuries, and we began conversing in the waiting room.

I had injured my back by trying to move a piano, which wasn't very interesting.

This woman had injured hers by trying to break her pet skunk's fall.

"She was a tiny baby when I got her," the woman said. "I found her out by our driveway, all alone, with her eyes still shut. How could I leave her there to die? I remembered the story of the Good Samaritan in the Bible. So, I took her inside, bought a baby animal feeder, and gave her formula every two hours for nearly a month."

"Every two hours? When did you sleep?" I asked.

"Oh, my kids helped me. We took turns eating,

sleeping, and feeding the skunk. It was a great bonding experience!"

"How did you hurt your back? Did you just get worn out, caring for the skunk?"

"No. After her eyes opened and she got big enough, I quit holding her on my lap when I fed her and put her on the kitchen counter. She's so lively, she jumps and plays all over the place. The other day she accidentally fell off the counter. When she fell, I didn't want her to get scared or hurt and spray everything, so I tried to grab her. Oooowww! I twisted my back. What's worse, I didn't catch her, and she sprayed like sixty."

"Oh, my goodness," I said.

"It really wasn't too strong," she said. "But from now on I'm keeping some tomato juice handy in case she does it again."

By now the therapists were ready for us. Throughout my treatment I thought about the lady with the skunk. I wanted to know more. Luckily, we got out of our treatments at the same time, and we met in the hallway.

"I must say I'm surprised anyone would take on the magnitude of your skunk project," I told her.

"I named her Marigold," she said. "Because she's like a bed of marigolds in the garden. Marigolds keep insects and other bothersome creatures away from the vegetables, you know."

We walked down the hall together.

"Here," she said. "Smell my sweater."

I sniffed her sleeve, which was definitely skunkish.

The skunk woman went on to say that she'd planned to have Marigold de-scented, but her friends told her she might get arrested for harboring a wild animal, so she decided against it.

"You mean you're keeping the skunk?" I asked as we entered the reception room.

"Sure. As long as I keep her happy, I shouldn't have any problems. But having a skunk for a pet sure is a challenge. Sorta like living with a time-bomb." She paid her bill at the receptionist's desk.

"Why not let Marigold return to the wild?" I wrote a check and then followed the woman out the door.

"Actually, Marigold is real helpful. My husband used to be a nice man, but in the last few years he's developed a terrible temper. After a couple of beers, he likes to push me around. Now that I have Marigold, Harry is as sweet as pie. I couldn't ask for a better man."

"He's afraid Marigold will spray him!"

"Marigold is more effective than an anger management class. Believe me, I know. Harry's tried counseling and even AA. But he didn't reform until I got Marigold."

By now we'd reached her vehicle, a fine and fancy SUV.

"Meet Marigold," she said, opening the front door on the passenger's side. She reached into the floorboard and pulled up a good-sized black and white squirming skunk, wearing a leash.

"You sweet thing," my new friend said to Marigold, kissing her on the top of her head.

"This is hard to believe," I told her, backing away. I watched as she put Marigold into an infant seat and strapped her in.

"All Marigold wants is peace and quiet. I'll bet she'd spray to high heaven if I accidentally had a wreck and she got hurt," my friend said. She reached down into her purse, pulled out a pair of doll-sized sunglasses and perched them on Marigold's nose. Marigold shook her head until the glasses fell off.

"She doesn't want to wear them. Never does," my friend said. She closed the door gently.

"Time to go pick up the kids," she said. "You'd be amazed how well they behave these days." Walking around to her side, she got in, started her SUV, and drove away.

After meeting the skunk woman and Marigold, I want to start a skunk ranch. I could make a lot of money and help humanity at the same time. Just think of it! Instead of sending thousands of soldiers to fight terrorists, we could send thousands of skunks! And I, no doubt, would get the government contract! Rich Mama!

What's more — instead of letting big kids bully little kids in our schools, we could pack a skunk in every little kid's backpack and the bullies would leave them alone. And instead of women and girls being harassed, assaulted and abducted by predators, they could rent skunk companions for protection.

And since Isis, Isil, Al Qaeda and Kim Jong Un refuse to get along with the rest of the world, the United

States could give them a deadline to curb their hatred. If they don't meet it, we'll release a million skunks into their strongholds. That'll provide some incentive to work together for World Peace.

Come to think of it, I'd send my biggest, baddest skunk to the White House, just to give our Commander-in-Chief his own personalized whiff of what George W. Bush once called "Shock and Awe."

At last, the powerless could hold their own against the powerful. What a concept. What a weapon. WMDs provided by Mother Nature, with no bloodshed involved.

I FEEL BAD ABOUT MY WHATCHAMACALLIT

The witty Hollywood screenwriter Nora Ephron once wrote a book titled, *I Feel Bad About my Neck*, in which she complained about the unattractiveness of aging. Once she was young and pretty; then she grew old. Poor thing.

I Feel Bad About My Neck was on the best-seller list for months.

I could write the same book, only better. Mine would read like an encyclopedia, and I'd list every part of me I feel bad about.

I feel rotten about my hair, forehead, wrinkles, eyes, jowls, skin, pores, teeth *and neck*. What's more, I feel lousy about my shoulders, elbows, arms, biceps and triceps. Recently I noticed that I've inherited my mother's swollen, spotted arthritic hands, and I feel horrible about it.

I'm heartbroken about my weak, crumbling fingernails.

I feel sad concerning my torso, back, hips, abs, cellulite, pasty flesh, knobby knees, varicose and spider veins, fallen arches, and horse-hoof toenails.

So there, Nora!

In between all those thoughts, I feel bad about my boobs and butt. My glutes and mammary glands, like flattened saddlebags, droop toward the floor.

I feel bad about my bones. About a hundred times a day I watch perky, pesky Hollywood starlets on television warn me about my brittle bones and recommend Boniva. Who knew I should have drunk milk and exercised all those years? If my bones are now brittle and thin, is it *my* fault?

I feel ghastly about my brain. Every day I spend a great deal of time wandering from room to room, not remembering where I am, who I am, or what I'm looking for. Takes forever to get dressed, find the car keys, and back out of the garage. I've been known to forget to raise the garage door. Then I *really* feel bad.

I'm more than a little irritated about my driving, cooking, housekeeping, and compulsive talking. I feel sad that I'm hard to get along with and that I insist I'm always right. I feel sorry that I overfed a family of goldfish when I was in the second grade, and they all died. I remember that particular incident better than whatever happened last week.

I have a whole lot more to feel morose about than Nora Ephron, who got stinking rich for mentioning her turkey-neck. Wait a minute – unfair. She already *was* stinking rich.

I feel lousy that I've gained a few pounds and lumber around like a sleepy bear, and when I put on a bathing suit, I look like a heavily veined beached albino whale. Kids at the swimming pool call me *Moby Dick*.

I feel bad that I feel bad about all these things.

So, give *me* the prize, Mr. Pulitzer! I feel really bad about getting so dadgum old.

But, on the other hand, I'm happy to still be alive. Unfortunately, the funny, talented Nora Ephron can't say the same thing. She and I were born the same year, in 1941, and she died of leukemia in 2012.

And that's where genuine sadness sets in. The loss of people we love and admire, the overwhelming holes, the gaps where they once were.

I feel terrible about the empty spaces.

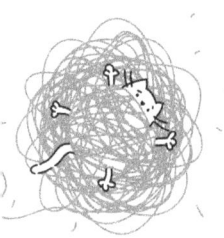

LEAPIN' LIZARDS!

"Leapin' Lizards!" exclaimed Little Orphan Annie of the comic strip by the same name, first penned in 1924. This was Annie's signature exclamation whenever she was frightened, shocked, disgusted or amazed.

"Arf!" answered her dog, Sandy, who always shared her opinions and adventures.

An orphan with a mop of red hair and vacant circles for eyes, Annie was taken in by Daddy Warbucks, who was a richer capitalist than Bill Gates, Warren Buffet, and all the Walmart Waltons combined. Unlike "The Donald," Oliver Warbucks had no hair, always wore a black suit, and was a serious-minded, but kind, stick-in-the-mud.

With his faithful servants Punjab – a turban-wearing eight-foot tall East Indian – and The Asp, who was an Asian, Daddy Warbucks helped Annie survive many a dangerous episode. Corrupt businessmen and villainous law-breakers abounded in those cartoon strips.

I never knew exactly what to make of Orphan Annie. When I was a kid, I admired her gusto, but it was clear she had no style. If she was adopted by the richest man in the country, why did she have only one dress, the little red number with the dinky white collar? Annie wore that same dress, white stockings, and Mary Jane shoes everywhere.

Why didn't she get a decent haircut? Surely her red nest hairdo could stand some thinning, shaping and straightening. And what was wrong with her eyes? With no pupils, could she even see? Why didn't the rich Warbucks spring for eyeglasses or, in later years, contact lens?

Although I didn't want to *look* like Annie, I wanted to *be* her. Since I was eager to have her adventures, I figured being an orphan wasn't a half-bad fate. To me, it was unfortunate that I had an intact family: a father, mother, a sister and a brother. How unlucky could a girl get? Not only did I have a family, but also – although I was plain-looking – I wasn't pitiful enough to attract the sympathies of a rich old geezer and his interesting sidekicks. What was worse, I had eyes.

Nevertheless, I went around exclaiming, "Leapin' lizards!" whenever I had a chance. And I made my family name our black and white spotted mongrel "Sandy."

What an entertaining comic strip! And compared with what we're mired down in today, what an age of innocence. Because, guess what? *Daddy Warbucks never tried to seduce Little Orphan Annie.* Neither did Punjab or The Asp. What a novelty: a decent father figure who had moral friends. Also, *Annie never wore plunging necklines, exposing extreme cleavage.* To my knowledge, she never even asked for a boob job. Since Annie was created in 1924, she's had ample time to get her figure re-adjusted. But a child of the Depression was never interested in breast enhancement (unlike the top-heavy hussy, Barbie). And as far as we know, *Annie always wore her underwear.* Today, some seriously maladjusted media stars forget to put their panties on before they climb into a limo and spread their legs. My grandmother called panties "step-ins." Well, I'm sure Annie always wore her step-ins.

To Annie, Punjab and The Asp were great pals, friends to depend on during episodes of international intrigue. They were loyal, trustworthy companions. Nobody was a racist. And nobody was a bully, except the villains.

Most of all, Annie never said the f- word. Imagine that. Nearly ninety years on this earth and pure of heart and language! And speaking of naughty language, how long has it been since you read a bestseller or went to a movie and weren't barraged by the f-word? Actually, every major character I've watched for the past year has said that previously forbidden word frequently.

Next time I head to the cinema, I'm taking a golf stroke counter, to click every time I hear it. The results should be posted on the internet and sent to Hollywood, to protest the writers' lack of imagination. In fact, I'd like movies to be rated not only according to sexual content, drug use, violence and language, but also how many times the characters use that particular offensive word.

My goodness. When I was growing up, that kind of language was so banned in our household I doubt my mother even knew what it meant. It was regarded so vile that if you saw it scrawled on a restroom wall, you were supposed to look at the floor, do your business, and get outta there.

Just think of it! Little Orphan Annie's catch phrase is "Leapin' lizards." *And speaking of leaping, wouldn't it be wonderful if filmmakers would leap into a general language and content revolution*? Wouldn't it be great if the most vile words and phrases were limited to killers and drug pushers who all died by the end of the movie? Then the other characters could leap into the revolution by using creative slang, such as, "Well butter my buns and call me a biscuit!"

And wouldn't it be *even better* if filmmakers would cut out the scenes of gratuitous sex and violence? Wouldn't it be marvelous if you could leave a theater feeling exhilarated and uplifted instead of wanting to crawl out with a paper bag over your head? Or slump out to the parking lot so depressed you could cut your throat?

Oh, well, "The sun'll come out tomorrow. Bet your bottom dollar.... Tomorrow, tomorrow, I love ya', tomorrow. You're only a day away."

I wish.

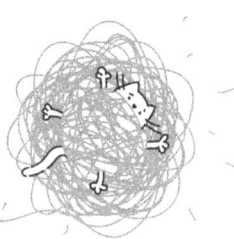

THE HUMILIATION CLINIC

The men in our lives may come and go, but our bodies are with us forever. And we'd jolly well better take care of them. The bodies, not the men.

When I was a child, later as a teenager, and then as a young woman, one medical doctor, old Dr. Gooch, pretty well took care of everything about me.

But now, as a result of aging and specialists, every part of my body is under the care of a different doctor. In other words, I'm divided up. Total strangers have drawn and quartered me, and not a single one of them would recognize me if we met at a cocktail party. Not that I'd want them to, because some of my parts are fairly gross. And exposing them to the human eye is humiliating. Still, I'd like to have a little more continuity in my health care.

I think every woman alive should have her own personal day of humiliation, whereby we expose all our private parts during an eight-hour clinic visit. The check-everything-on-the-old-broad's–body clinic that takes care of it all. Here's the way it would work:

Stop eating food at least twelve hours before Your Special Day of Humiliation. Drink some awful stuff that makes you go to the bathroom for hours.

On the morning of your appointment, your first stop is the dermatologist, who examines your hair, wrinkles, warts and moles and pronounces you fit to live another year. I'm talking here about health, honey, not beauty. The doctors that make you beautiful are a different breed altogether.

Next, *hie thee* to the internist, who listens to your vitals and takes a little blood, plus a sample or two of yuck.

No food.

Git along little doggie to the audiologist, then the ophthalmologist, then the dentist and the cardiologist. Take a stress test.

It's mid-day. Skip lunch.

By the time you have a mammogram you won't have the energy to be nervous or embarrassed. Just lean against the machine in zombie fashion, and it'll all be over in a jiff.

Still no food.

Next, the gynecologist, who probably won't be charming. Hopefully, you won't be like my friend, Tammy Sue, who got set up in stirrups and then was forgotten while the whole staff went to lunch. An hour later, the nurse walked in and shrieked with surprise when she found poor Tammy still there, sedately draped, feet in stirrups, as mad as a cat on steroids.

With any luck, that won't happen to you.

Now visit the podiatrist, who no doubt will tell you you've ruined your feet from wearing pointy toes, tight boots, high-heeled shoes and sandals. Let him fit you for orthopedics.

No food.

See a chiropractor, who'll inform you that, through the years, you've lifted, strained, and carried flower pots and children all wrong. Feel him stretch the heck out of your spine.

No food.

Last, get that little old colonoscopy. By now you're too weak, hungry, and worn out to care who sees what.

And very last, have someone drive you home, serve you a sizzling steak, an overloaded potato, and a glass of fine red wine. Then let that someone tuck you in bed. It's over for another year.

Now that's my idea of a clinic of Hungry Humiliation. But I'm all for it. A day of repentance, or spiritual re-awakening, something to put on your calendar at the first of each year.

Schedule at your convenience this annual day of dread, nervousness, and stomach-in-knots embarrassment. Only one day to possibly have to hear the words we all fear: "I'm sorry, my dear, I've found a lump."

And if that happens, suddenly you'll be so scared you won't be hungry again for a long time.

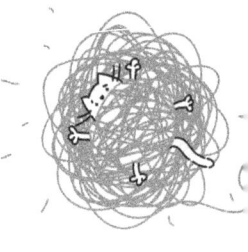

I DREAMED I KISSED SANTA CLAUS

I dreamed I kissed Santa Claus…in my Maidenform bra.

How many people out there remember the Maidenform bra ads? Or am I the only old broad that spent a lackluster, bony, flat-chested childhood mooning over pictures of gorgeous models having grand adventures in their brassieres?

These ads, which ran in magazines from 1949 until 1969, featured scrumptious settings and beautiful models posed appropriately for particular, exciting events. In each ad, the model wore absolutely nothing from her shoulders to her waist, except a white, double-pointed, wide-strapped Maidenform bra.

Here are a few examples:

"I dreamed I went to the opera … in my Maidenform bra." (Model wears long formal skirt, elbow-length gloves, pearls and bra at the opera house.)

"I dreamed I danced a ballet … in my Maidenform bra." (Dressed in pink tutu and bra, the model pirouettes across a stage on *Pointe*.)

"I dreamed I barged down the Nile … in my Maidenform bra." (Wearing Cleopatra costume, King Tut jewelry, and bra, the model paddles her canoe.)

"I dreamed I was WANTED … in my Maidenform bra." (A tough, Jane Russell look-alike totes two six shooters as she grins from under a large cowboy hat. Her bra is big, Baby.)

Growing up with these ads, I believed I could accomplish anything. All I needed was an amply endowed chest and a Maidenform bra. No education, no training would be necessary for me to be like one of the girls in the ads. Adventurous girls who dreamed they "had the world on a string," "painted the town red," "stopped traffic," "fought a bull," and "swayed the jury."

What's more, one Maidenform model dreamed she was a jack-in-the-box, and another dreamed she was a "knock-out." One girl dreamed she was bookends, which I always thought was a little weird, because a bookend implies no action at all, just a heavy bottom.

In short, these ads were interesting, because they showed gals doing important things – in their dreams, and in their underwear.

Here's my favorite: A pretty model with lots of lipstick and black mascara leans off the side of a fire engine, hanging onto a ladder with one hand and waving with the other. She wears a red helmet, black patent leather boots, red satin shorts trimmed with rhinestones, shiny white gloves, and, of course, her brassiere.

The caption reads, "I dreamed I went to blazes in my Maidenform bra."

Listen, girls, if you missed looking at these ads in every magazine you picked up when you were a kid, you missed a jolly good world of fantasy and fun.

And unfortunately for gals like me, someone in the NYC advertising world decided these ads were sexy, vulgar, alarmingly sexist and just no darned good.

So, what do we have now? Today the bra has lost its luster, its mystery. Now, rock stars wear their bras out in public. The sight of celebrity cleavage has become absolutely Ho Hum. Exposure of the human mammary glands has become so common we can't get away from it. For instance, the female contestants in "Dancing with the Stars" wear diminutive bras as well as skinny thongs as they shake it out all over the dance floor. My friends and I watch these women in their skimpy costumes and wonder aloud when some invisible string is going to break and leave a girl totally exposed. That may be one of the thrills of watching the stars dance.

So, if bosoms are getting boring now, what was the thrill of the Maidenform bra ads for twenty years? What was the point? No pun intended.

The point was always fantasy. Not sex, not sexism, but fantasy. In a not-very-nice world of disappointment and pain, human beings have always needed fantasy. If you don't believe me, just check out the cave men's drawings.

When we enter the holiday season, we approach a magical time for hopes, wishes and dreams. Regardless of a person's religious persuasion, surely everyone agrees that Christmas is a beautiful time for creativity and fantasy.

I dreamed I flew with reindeer … in my Maidenform bra.

I dreamed I danced as the Sugarplum Fairy … in my Maidenform bra.

I dreamed I played the Ghost of Christmas Past … in my Maidenform bra.

I dreamed I sang "White Christmas" … in my Maidenform bra.

Some people say that surely God didn't have all this secularism in mind when he planned the First Christmas. These same people say that what we have done to his birthday would make Jesus want to drink soapy water.

I don't know about that. Most Americans probably do celebrate a secular Christmas to the extreme. But these same people are the first to reach for their checkbooks whenever they hear of others who need help, people struck down by tragedy all over the globe.

Sometimes razzle-dazzle and generosity go hand in hand.

As superficial as we seem, we're all aware of the harsh realities of our broken world. And personally, I don't know anyone who doesn't wish, hope and pray for Peace on Earth, Good Will to All Humankind.

Especially Peace.

I dreamed I helped save a Sudanese family and kissed Santa Claus on the same day … in my red and green silk Maidenform bra.

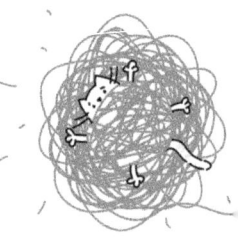

AIN'T NO CURE FOR THE SUMMERTIME BLUES

It's the dog days of summer, and practically everybody I know is in a bad mood. Turn on the television news for only ten minutes, and you'll lose your Little Miss Sunshine personality. You can't help it. The state of affairs in our country and the rest of the world can make you PDC (pretty darned cynical).

Go to Hallmark for a cheerful message to send to yourself for a burst of laughter, and you'll find rows of cards featuring that cynical old grouch, Maxine. Although Maxine and her pit-bull-looking dog are humorous, their messages are seriously mean. She's one rude little old lady.

Go shopping at a lovely gift store, and you may find a fancy plaque that reads, "What if the Hokey Pokey really *is* what it's all about?"

Not a happy thought.

Call your best friend in another state, and you'll hear a woeful account of a) the droughts, b) the floods, c) the wildfires, d) her dog's death, or e) her villainous husband leaving her for another woman.

All these events can practically shovel you under.

I, for one, have never been so et up with grouchiness. What exactly is causing this rotten mood? Is it the war or is it the weather? The collapsed bridge in Minneapolis or all those movie stars having to serve time in the pokey? (Actually, I don't really care about the rich and famous going to jail; I just resent having to hear about it.)

If the terrorists don't get us, then e-coli, lead-painted toys, drug-addicted criminals, Washington scoundrels, our out-dated infra-structure, or wild young female drivers will.

As Charlie Brown would say, "Aaaauurrgh!!!"

Fortunately, I've found an activity that helps me make it through the night – and the day.

When the going gets tough, the tough get going to the movies. We can escape our falling-bridge phobia and our global-warming guilt by watching flicks. Works better than a psychiatrist. No foolin.'

This psycho-aid, however, doesn't work so well with home rental movies. It's more therapeutic to sit in a cool dark theater with a horde of polite strangers (cell-phones off, please! And don't rattle those candy wrappers!) and enjoy mutual entertainment with the rest of humanity.

If you're feeling low, go to see *Ocean's Thirteen*. Not only does the plot demand constant attention (hereby causing you to forget your troubles), but also George Clooney is ONE HANDSOME HUNK. Eye Candy.

With his long eyelashes and little-boy grin, George

is so angelically gorgeous he looks like he's already died and gone to heaven. He alone is worth a seven-dollar sack of popcorn.

Or, if you're suffering from boredom and you crave adventure, go to see *Rescue Dawn*. You'll be riveted by the action and amazed at the ingenuity of the main character, played by Christian Bale. You'll be so glad you're not a prisoner of war in Laos that you'll want to celebrate after the film by swigging down a gigantic margarita, thereby getting a gigantic headache.

But it's a happy headache.

Or go to see *Hairspray*. Not only does this film have a great social message and wonderful 60's music and fashions, but also John Travolta is hilarious, singing and dancing in drag.

And the huge back-combed hairdos! As they say in Texas, "The higher the hair, the closer to God." According to this theology, everybody in *Hairspray* is headed for the heavenly gates.

Or, if you really want to enter another world for a while, take a child to see *Ratatouille*. Making a charming hero out of a rat isn't easy, and the film is a wonder. For adults, hearing children laughing at the adventures of likeable rodents is great fun.

Let's face it. If we could bottle children's laughter and give it out like free medicine, maybe we could save the world.

Even if you haven't become totally depressed by the events of this summer, the movies provide great therapy for the ordinary late-summer dog-day doldrums. The song says, "There ain't no cure for the summertime blues." That may be true, but a good movie can cheer you up, at least for a little while.

Au revoir. I'm off to the theater. I'm headed to *The Bourne Ultimatum*, starring that sensitive good-lookin' darling, Matt Damon. See you at the flicks, Chicks.

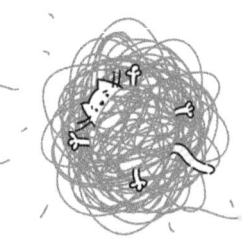

THE DEVIL CARRIES PRADA

Everybody in this entire country is getting ready for school. From college students, who pack computers and CD players into their snazzy automobiles, to three-year-olds, who put snacks and extra underwear into small brightly colored backpacks. From salespeople stocking school supplies, to bookstore owners ordering textbooks, to parents whipping out their charge cards to buy necessary items for their children, everyone has joined the Back to School Brigade.

It sorta makes me feel left out. Somehow, I want to join them. Do something to expand my horizons. Take a class or two. Get organized. Start a project. Learn something new or teach someone a different and worthwhile subject.

I recently read a great article by a woman named Amy Sutherland, who has written a book about training exotic animals. (*Kicked, Bitten and Scratched: Life and Lessons at the Premier School for Exotic Animal Trainers*)

Ms. Sutherland spent many hours observing the teaching techniques of trainers of hyenas, cougars, dolphins, and baboons. The idea is that if you're patient enough and willing to spend an inordinate amount of time at it, you can teach an animal to do almost anything. You give rewards and you withhold affection appropriately and even an old dolphin will practically beg you to let him perform.

Amy Sutherland was so taken with the results of these methods that she decided to try them on her husband, the typical alpha American male. And what do you know? The methods worked.

Not owning a dolphin or any other exotic animal, I decided to use the same techniques to teach my husband a few tricks. Nothing complicated, just three simple activities: lower the potty seat, throw away trash mail and newspapers, and never, ever, under any circumstance, ask me where anything is.

Training was going well until I made the mistake of telling my bunko group about my project. Everybody hooted and hurrahed, and before I knew it, they'd all gone home and told their husbands that I was treating my husband like a dumb animal. Their husbands told my alpha male, and he confronted me about it.

"That's not true," I told him. "I'm not treating you like a dumb animal. I'm treating you like a dolphin. In the animal kingdom, a dolphin is considered practically a genius. You should be flattered."

So, the cat was out of the bag, so to speak. I *was* treating him like an animal, and my training took a definite turn for the worse. When friends in our chummy neighborhood teased him even more about it, he told me to quit the training. What's more, he said, he would continue to do those things that practically drive me to despair. The only way I can stop his raised seat, piles of newspapers, and "Where is the (fill in the blank)?" behavior is to kill him.

And murder is not an option.

So, I'm starting a new Project.

This time, I'm trying to reform and organize *myself*. And I'm starting by organizing the stuff I carry with me all the time. A handbag with specific pockets and compartments would be just the ticket! I need a new handbag to keep everything decent and in order. It's the hopeful Presbyterian in me.

Think about all the stuff the average American woman lugs around with her, and you'll agree it's an amazing phenomenon that we don't have fractured backs and twitchy shoulders. If I can find the perfect handbag, I'll write an article for *The American Chiropractic Journal*, sharing the good news.

Oh, I have plenty of handbags in my closet, but not one of them is perfect. Some are shaped like sacks, and everything lands in a deep pile at the bottom. Some are narrow, with square corners, and when filled up they don't close quite right. One, an evening bag shaped like a flask, is totally inappropriate for every occasion except New Year's Eve. And my expensive funeral bag, a tailored black leather envelope, is so small it holds only one handkerchief. I have handbags in every color and every size, made from every material, genuine and fake.

I hate them all. I can never find my cell phone, my lipstick, or my car keys. And I'm sick of groping around in my purse all the time, like some weird old harridan headed for the booby hatch.

Years ago, I went to see the movie *The Devil Wears Prada.* In this light little comedy Meryl Streep plays the boss from hell, Miranda Priestly. It's true that Miranda is as mean as a witch straight out of Shakespeare. Her husband, poor man, finally leaves her, and she has no friends. But she has a wardrobe to die for.

In scene after scene, Miranda arrives at work and tosses her coat AND HER DESIGNER HANDBAG (a different one every day) on the desk of her assistant. I must have counted at least twenty handbag scenes. With all those Chanel, Gucci, Prada, and Kelly bags, the film probably cost millions of dollars in handbag inventory alone.

Any one of those ten thousand-dollar little numbers would be perfect for me. I'd gladly give up the many ugly, pitifully not-right handbags in my closet for one of Miranda's. Sell my soul to the devil and give me a designer handbag.

If you hear about a *Devil Wears Prada* handbag contest or charity auction, please let me know. I'd like to be the charity to which one of Meryl Streep's mighty fine purses is donated.

Unfortunately, until I can get myself a super-purse, I'll probably just stick with my old chaotic mess.

In the meantime, I'm looking for an exotic animal to help me organize my household. Something with opposable thumbs, perhaps a small monkey. I have a neat little toilet seat trick to teach him.

PECKED TO DEATH

Recently, while browsing through a gift shop in Fredericksburg, Texas, I saw a large plaque that read, "Living with teenagers is like being pecked to death by a chicken."

I'd like to add to that thought: Living with a teenager during the SUMMERTIME is like being pecked to death by a whole flock of chickens every livelong day.

In many ways, teenagers try to drive us crazy. One problem for parents is it's hard to live up to their expectations. We adults let them down. We disappoint them. They don't like our looks, can't stand our stories, don't laugh at our jokes, and constantly bombard us with requests for More! More! More!

"I'm bored. What's there to do? Is there anything to eat? Yuk! I don't like that! Why can't I, like, stay out all night with my friends? We're not going to DO anything! Give me one good reason! Everyone else is going! I want a new car! You are, like, the worst, cruelest mother in the whole world! I need money. Now! Yes, I'm, like, wearing this outfit in like, public! What's wrong with it? Huh? Huh? Huh?" Cry and whine.

My mother used to say, "Don't sass me, young lady. You're grounded!"

But today if you try to discipline a teenager, he just curls his lip, grabs his car keys and runs out the door.

Not only are teenagers a tad rude at times, but also most of them are very messy all the time. For instance, they leave their dirty laundry everywhere.

Last week I attended a religious meeting at the lovely home of my best friend, Tammy Sue Rocker. Our Bible study group had invited a minister to explain the book of *Deuteronomy*. We wanted to know what was up with the Hebrews and why they felt it was O.K. to run around the Promised Land murdering everybody. All that violence! All that gore!

As the minister sat in an easy chair, his feet got entangled in something sticking out from under his chair: Tammy Sue's daughter's thong underwear.

The preacher talked about God, Moses and the Israelites, but none of us heard a word. We were too busy watching his shiny black shoes thrashing in the flesh-colored lacy mini-panty. He was totally unaware that his feet had a problem, and none of us were about to tell him.

When he finished explaining the book of *Deuteronomy*, he stood up, tried to take a step, got a little off-balance, and finally looked down at the tangled thong wrapped around his ankles. Yelping, he jumped straight up and when he landed, he stomped on it. Then he kicked it across the room as if it were a snake.

It wasn't a religious moment.

But that's a good example of how a thoughtless teenager can ruin a spiritual event and humiliate a preacher at the same time.

Years ago, when my sisters and I were driving my mother crazy, she'd say, "You're going through a phase, and I hope I live long enough to see you get through it." I've told my teenagers the same thing.

Reading this, a person might think I don't like teenagers. Not true. Imagine a woman who put up with her own lazy lounge lizards at home and at the same time taught other parents' adolescents in the classroom. For years, that was me. I actually like the little buggers. But I understand their wily ways.

So, hang in there! Vacation time is nearly over. And in these dog days of summer, let's do our best to put up with our whiney, cell phone addicted, text messaging, hormone-crazed whippersnappers.

Because listen, Mother girlfriends, there's a pay-off. These acne-faced, navel-exposing, beer guzzling, tattoo-enhanced, possibly pot smoking, computer worshipping, fast driving, surly, eyebrow piercing, selfish, hostile, disrespectful pea-brains in nearly grown-up bodies will eventually mature and become someone you actually enjoy having dinner with.

They'll reproduce, and they'll give you your own set of absolutely perfect grandchildren. And your precious grandbabies will evolve into ghastly teenagers who perform their own chicken-pecking routine on these kids who are currently driving you nuts.

Ah, retribution.

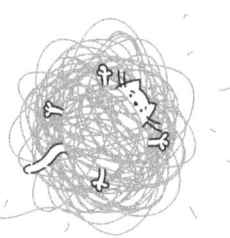

MEN ARE LIKE GRAPES

A friend of mine gave me a darling package of cocktail napkins. Each napkin reads, "Men are like a fine wine. They start out as grapes. It's our job to stomp on them until they mature into something you would like to have dinner with."

Ain't it the truth, honey.

Last year during the holidays, this package of napkins gave me hope and inspiration. While shopping, decorating, and wrapping gifts, I entertained secret thoughts about reforming, or "putting the stomp," on my husband.

I used to stomp him pretty well, but in the last few years I've gotten lax, and he isn't even close to being fine wine. Instead, he's still a messy old grape.

The idea of reforming a man comes with the territory in the family I grew up in. My mother used to tell my sisters and me, "Girls, a husband is like a Christmas tree. While looking for a tree, you go out into the forest and surround yourself with all sizes, shapes, and varieties of evergreens. Then you choose one and cut it down. You bring it home and get to work. You water it, prune it, and decorate it. The more you trim the tree, the better it looks and the more you love it."

"But a Christmas tree eventually turns brown and dies," my youngest sister, the literal one, argued.

"Not if you water it and make it think it's happy," Mother reasoned. "Listen, girls, what I'm saying is this: Men are trainable. Like puppies. You just must keep after them all the time. Be vigilant and keep a newspaper handy."

"What will we train men to do?" asked my sister.

"Honey, you'd be surprised. Why, some men pick up their dirty socks and throw away old newspapers. Some empty the trash and know how to cook. Some can load a dishwasher and make up a bed. Some even put down toilet seats!"

"What happened to Dad?" we asked. "He's not very well trained."

"I got a little lazy," she admitted. "Consequently, I lost control. That's why I'm telling you this now. So, you'll be prepared."

I'm sure my mother would love the analogy of men as grapes being stomped into fine wine.

Do you remember the famous segment of *I Love Lucy*, when Lucy and Ethyl are in a tub of grapes, dressed as gypsies, slipping and sliding in grape goo? It's an unforgettable scene in television history, which has given me courage. Stomping my husband into fine wine might be a sloppy project, but in the end, it'll be well worth it.

To accomplish my goals, I presented my husband with his list of New Year's Resolutions:

1. I will stop littering and making outrageous messes all over the house.
2. I will stop snoring and keeping my loving wife awake all night.
3. I will stop complaining about my wife's high maintenance expenditures.

"Sign this, please," I told him. "It's historic. You're living in the midst of a revolution."

The man looked at me with puzzlement. "I don't do any of these things," he said.

"Oh, no?" I asked. I went to my closet and grabbed a pair of high-heeled boots. Then I pulled them on and started strutting and singing:

These boots are made for stomping,
and that's just what they'll do.
One of these days they're gonna start
and stomp all over you.

"O K," he said. "You win." Then he retreated into his inner sanctum of a home office, which closely resembles a pigsty. He took the list of resolutions with him.

In a few minutes, he returned.

"I have my own list," he told me. "Read my resolutions for *you*, and if *you're* willing to change *your* ways, we'll both sign these papers. We'll even have them notarized."

"You want *me* to change *my* ways? You must be kidding!"

"Honey, you're not perfect."

"My mother thought I was."

"Your mother was a Nazi."

His list of resolutions was unrealistic.

1. I will start cooking.

2. I will start being pleasant 24/7.

3. I will start cutting back on all expenditures.

"Look," I told him, "I'm not trying for the 'fine wine' award. *You* are."

"Against my will," he said.

"Well, I'm not gonna cook. I'm not gonna smile all the time like some deranged Dale Carnegie cheerleader. And I'm not gonna give up shopping."

"We're at a stand-off," he said. Then he added, "Why don't we throw away those cocktail napkins? They've caused a lot of trouble."

"Better yet, let's have a cocktail," I told him.

"What do you want to drink?" he asked.

"A glass of fine wine."

The designer of the darling napkins was wrong. Men really aren't like grapes. My mother was wrong, also. Men aren't like Christmas trees or puppies, either.

Instead, they're like sweet, housebroken weasels.

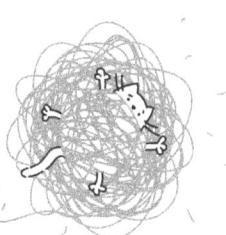

RAISE YOUR GLASS TO MOTHERHOOD

On this Mother's Day, I'd like to propose a toast. Here's to the *young mother*:

- the frightened teenager;
- the busy soccer mom;
- the single mother stretched to the limit;
- the carpool organizer;
- the homeroom mother;
- the corporate exec who calls 911 for a colicky baby;
- the *La Leche* believer who's unable to breastfeed;
- the *La Leche* believer with a busy breast pump;
- the good sport who stays with sick kids while their dad plays golf;
- the mother of a child with special needs;
- the mom waiting in the snow for a school bus;
- the one carrying a briefcase;

- the woman who weeps for her lost baby;
- and the one who adopts a child.

Here's to the *middle-aged mother*:

- the one who finds her son's stash of marijuana;
- the home-schooling mother;
- the worried mother, waiting up late;
- the one who buys nothing for herself, but takes her kids to piano and dance lessons instead;
- the gal who sits in pouring rain to watch her boy or girl play ball;
- the perfectionist mother;
- the sandwich generation mother;
- the mother of the bride, determined to host the perfect wedding;
- the mother of the groom, determined to wear beige and keep her mouth shut;
- the disappointed mother, whose child is in trouble;
- the proud mother, applauding at graduation;
- and the brave mother who sends her child to war.

Here's to the *older mother*:

- the one who stitches quilts;
- the one who bakes cakes and fries chicken over a hot stove;
- the mother who has outlived one of her children;

- the woman who wonders when the kids will call;
- the reader of nursery rhymes to grandchildren;
- the grandmother who accepts young-motherly duties all over again;
- the mother who backs off and lets her children travel their own road;
- the one who feels lousy but doesn't complain;
- the depressed lady;
- the laughing, story-telling entertainer;
- the mother who reads the Bible;
- and the one who's angry at God.

Here's to Chinese mothers, forced to give up their baby girls; African grandmothers, taking in grandchildren whose parents have died of AIDS; and East Indian mothers, whose little ones are starving. And here's to the mothers in the Middle East. All of them.

Let's toast all the mothers who worry that they're not smart enough, patient enough, organized enough, resourceful enough, brave enough, loving enough, lucky enough or tough enough to do a decent job of rearing their children.

Let's hear it for the sleep-deprived and the cell-phone addicted, in ghettos and in beach houses, gay mothers and straight, hot flashing and line-dancing.

So, girlfriend, raise a glass to motherhood. It's the hardest job you'll ever love.

THE CAPTAIN'S TABLE

My eleven best friends and I took a Mediterranean cruise last summer. We cooked up the whole trip one winter night while playing bunko and swigging sangria. A few days later, we decided on the date, booked the cruise, and bought the tickets. Bought skimpy swimsuits (mostly bikinis), swishy skirts, and tight shorts. One chick even got her navel pierced. Another got an ankle tattoo. Collectively, we waxed, exfoliated, tanned, highlighted, pumped iron, lost weight, tucked tummies, and even endured a shot or two of Botox. All of this to prove that we're glamorous American women. And all this not to be outdone by each other. Then we left our jobs, husbands, boyfriends, children and elderly nagging parents behind.

The plan was to tool around the Mediterranean Sea for a couple of weeks, docking at various interesting places and hotspots. We'd look at ruins and nude statues and we'd shop, shop, shop. At night, while cruising, we'd eat, sleep, and play bunko. When it came to dealing with men, the single chicks would be on the alert for stray flirty guys, but we married ones would be content to read trashy novels. The trip would be adventurous, educational, and fattening. We were up for it. We were excited and perky. We were the best of friends.

Trouble was, we ran into an obstacle, in the form of the drop-dead-gorgeous captain.

From the moment he said "Hello," he had every last one of us. Honestly, he was a double-dash darling man — tall, dark, swarthy, mysterious and sexy, strutting around in his navy-blue captain's suit, greeting everybody and smiling. Give me a handsome man in a uniform, and my knees buckle automatically. He was a real hottie.

Although some of us were married, some divorced, some widowed, and some forever single, we all fell in love with the captain. Everybody wanted his attention, and when he appeared, we'd announce, "Captain Sighting!"

If he'd been Elvis Presley risen from the dead, we couldn't have been more excited!

"Easy on the eyes," we agreed. "Probably hard on the heart."

"Eye candy," we salivated.

Tammy, the English teacher, began quoting "O, Captain, My Captain," by Walt Whitman:

O Captain! My Captain! Our fearful trip is done!
The ship has weather'd every rack, the prize we sought is won.

She quoted old Walt at least twenty times a day, which made me want to smack her.

Nancy, a single attorney, made the first move on the captain by inviting him to play bunko. When he wavered, she challenged him to play a marathon of games. He declined and ran away to his quarters.

Desiree, a divorcée and my roommate, wanted to have a date with him and talked about it constantly.

"Wonder what he's like?" she whispered. "I mean *really*. I wonder what he's *really* like."

Everybody in our group wanted something from him, and everyone schemed to get his attention. We stopped being such good friends.

I acted no better than the rest of these hussies. I wanted to be the first to have an actual conversation with the gorgeous hunk. I wanted to interview him.

So, we all wanted something, but the one thing we had in common was that we all wanted to sit at the Captain's Table.

The captain had a charming Hungarian accent, which made our hearts thump with passion. He got his *v*'s and *w*'s mixed up in a truly seductive way. One day I spied him on the stairway and made a beeline toward him. I asked if I could interview him for an article I'd write when I got back to America.

"Oh, I don't know," he said. "Thank you wary much, but I don't speak English vell enough."

"Your English is great," I countered. "Just let me ask you a few questions. I can meet you any time, any place. Preferably in private."

"I hear that American reporters don't alvays tell the

truth," he said, smiling.

"You mean we *embellish*? I'd never do that. I only jazz things up a little to make them more interesting," I answered.

"Vell," he said, "I vouldn't vant you to jazz *me* up."

"Oh, please, Captain! Just a teeny-weeny interview!"

"Vell, I think about it."

From then on, every time I walked up to him, he said, "I'm still thinking." So, I finally blew off my interview plan.

One night my roommate, Desiree, showered, washed and curled her hair, put on fresh make-up, and then donned her gown and robe. Looking up from my trashy novel, I watched her.

She said, "I really can't go to sleep just yet. Think I'll stroll around the deck before I turn in."

"You're in your nightgown! Are you crazy?" I asked.

"Well, I might accidentally meet somebody," she answered.

"The captain? You're out of your mind!"

"I'm not talking about shacking up forever," she said. "I'm just talking about tonight." She opened the cabin door and left.

I was so furious with her I could hardly concentrate on the juicy stuff in my book.

In a few minutes, Desiree returned.

"Well?" I asked.

"I saw the captain. He said I scared him. He thought I was a ghost. Now I ask you – Do I look like a ghost?"

"You look like a lunatic that's just escaped from an asylum," I told her.

Day after day, we watched the captain. But he wouldn't have anything to do with us, and he didn't issue any invitations to the Captain's Table. And every night he had some sluggish unattractive married couple sitting at his table with him. Old and totally boring. Why wouldn't he invite some of us?

"It's because we're all so cute and fascinating he can't decide which ones to ask," Cindy, the stockbroker, said.

"Actually, it's because he thinks we're crazy," I said.

One evening, after a day of heavy rain, the captain called the entire shipload of tourists together. Over a hundred and fifty people gathered in the lounge. Nervously, he explained that a summer storm was approaching. It was dangerous for us to lollygag in the Mediterranean at such a leisurely pace, so he was heading for port as quickly as possible. Full steam ahead. There we would disembark and live in a hotel, thus cutting our cruise short.

"The vater is up too high and the vaves are too rough," he said. "Ve aren't safe. Tonight, vhen you go to bed, have your life jackets vithin reach. And sleep with your waluables. If you have something wary, wary waluable, put it inside your fanny packet and vear it vile you sleep."

Hearing the captain say "Fanny packet" made us laugh. We twelve women sat in the lounge snorting and giggling while our shipmates stared at us, shaking their heads and grumbling to each other,

"Brazen!"

"Wild women!"

"Obnoxious twits!"

We were so totally undignified. Still, the captain's concern about our safety and our waluables made us love him even more. Each one of us felt more passion for him, and we quivered with hilarious desire.

After hearing the captain's bad news and making utter fools of ourselves, we headed for the dining room. It would be our last night on board with the captain. Thus far, he'd done nothing – absolutely zilch – to fulfill any of our dreams. No encouragement whatsoever. And we hadn't played a decent round of bunko for fretting about him and his whereabouts. All of us, trying to wriggle an invitation out of him, had become a nest of competitive witches. We could hardly stand each other.

"O Captain, My Captain—" Tammy proclaimed, as we sat at our table and ordered drinks from the waiter.

"Listen," I said. "I'm sick of everybody moaning over the captain. Girls, we've acted like over-heated cats! No wonder Europeans don't like us. We're ridiculous!"

"You're right!" said Desiree. "He isn't worth it! He thought *I* was a *ghost*! Ooops!" She realized she'd let the others know about her designs on the captain.

"Let's just have fun tonight," Nancy said. "After dinner, we'll play a round of mindless bunko before we go to our cabins to pack our waluables." Laughing, we ordered our entrees and settled down for our last meal on board.

"Ladies –" a voice said. We looked up. It was the captain. "May I join you?" he asked. All twelve of us scooted over, while the waiters set another place at our huge table. We were so surprised we were speechless. No one said a word.

"Vonderful," he said, looking around at us and smiling. "I'll have the weal," he told the waiter, settling back in his chair. "Vith Wegetables."

Having dinner with twelve crazy American broads was his act of charity. The threatening weather was doing him a favor by getting us off his ship. Tomorrow he'd be happy to tell us goodbye. I could tell from his gorgeous Hungarian gypsy-like grin.

CPSIA information can be obtained
at www.ICGtesting.com
Printed in the USA
LVHW091417231219
641445LV00002B/210/P

Made in the USA
Middletown, DE
30 June 2018

- If someone is being bullied at school would you let them sit with you at lunch or sit with you on the bus if you ride one?

Circle one
Yes or No   Why or why not?

- How do you think someone who is being bullied feels?

_____
_____
_____
_____
_____
_____
_____
_____

Stopping the bull

- If you were being bullied what are two things you can do about it?

1. _____

2. _____

- What are three things you can do to help someone who is being bullied?

1. _____

2. _____

3. _____

Resources

For more resources on Bullying

www.Antibullying.net

www.StopBullying.gov

www.NoBullying.com

A few tips for kids.

- Treat everyone with respect
- Stand up for others
- Don't keep your feelings to yourself.
- Talk to a trusted adult
- Stay away from places where bullying occurs.

Rhyming Social Stories
Mary Lee Kendal

A Pig in a Wig - Anti-Bullying

The Goat on a Boat - Overcoming Shyness

Why Can't I - have a cell phone yet?

Be the first to know about new releases, discounts, promotions & events @ www.MaryLeeKendal.com

Follow us on Social Media

www.MaryLeeKendal.com
www.MaryLeeKendal.com/ToyStore
www.Facebook.com/MaryLeeKendal
www.Instagram.com/MaryLeeKendal
www.Pinterest.com/MaryLeeKendal

Please leave a review

The Pig in a Wig
by Mary Lee Kendal

Thank you for reading "The Pig in a Wig."
If you enjoyed this rhyming social story can you please leave a review on the Amazon page for this book?

Pretty please ☺

It will take less than one minute and I would personally appreciate it.

It will help other young readers discover this book and learn about anti bullying. If each day one child stood up for someone being bullied, our world would be a better place.

Thank You
Mary Lee Kendal

That night, Penelope put away her wig
and stared at her ears that seemed so big.
She felt like she wanted to cry.
Her heart felt sad like a smashed cherry pie.

Penelope had been mean
to her friend, for sure.
Just like the other animals
had been mean to her.

Penelope knew what she had to do.
She'd apologize right away, when the day became new.
She would jump right to it,
and throw her wig away too.
She was going to be herself, yes sir,
Because her ears were perfect,
just as they were.

Her friend, Polly noticed the new wig. And she noticed that it covered the ears that were so big.

But she also noticed that Penelope was a whole different pig.

"Penelope, your ears are perfect just as they are."

"You don't need to change anything to be a super star."

"Just be yourself and you'll always go far."

Penelope laughed at her friend. She didn't want this day to end.

"So what if I am a pig that's wearing a wig?"

"At least no one is teasing me about my ears that are so big."

"And that is what I want today."

She pointed at her friend.

"Now you go away!"

She went outside and played a game of tag.
She won a game of Capture the Flag.
It was so much fun to zig and then zag.

But, not today.
No one looked at her ears that were big.
No one even looked at her new wig.
Penelope felt like dancing the great pig jig.

At lunch, nice words began to come Penelope's way.
"I really like your hair today."
"Would you like to come outside and play?"

The animals had never said these things before.
It was like the wig had opened a brand-new door.
Penelope loved this feeling and wanted more.

Penelope made it to school.
Not hearing those mean words
was pretty cool.
She sat at her desk, still waiting for
something cruel.

The school bell rang with a clang.
All the animals rushed
to their desks with a bang.
Penelope sat quietly and felt sort of sad,
As this is when her day usually gets bad.

They always point and they laugh.
They make fun of my ears.
I frown, hang my head,
And nobody cares.

Penelope sighed.
Then sighed again.
It was time for her day to begin.

She walked down the sidewalk.
She listened to the animals talk.
Waiting and waiting for someone to gawk.

Every step,
Brought Penelope more pep.
No one was talking about her ears.
It felt so good
not to worry about those fears.

Penelope Pig stared at her wig.
"It should cover my ears."
"Everyone says they're so big."

Penelope put on her wig, but
didn't feel like dancing the jig.
Her big ears were still there.
It just didn't seem fair.

"No one else needs to cover up their ears."
"And no one else comes running home in tears."

A Pig in a Wig; an anti-bullying rhyming social story for young readers.

Penelope Pig is having a wonderful day.
But, it didn't always go that way.
Sometimes the other kids would make fun of her.
She was tired of it that was for sure.
She set out to change who she was.
Polly reminds her she is special just because.

Special Thanks

Thank you divine spirit and the magic of the universe, thank you for peanut butter and beaches, weber grills, language and puppies, and for the children to enjoy them. Thank you for my family and friends who love and support all of my endeavors and to Judy who lets me be me.

Thank you to all the parents and kids who have stood up to bullies. Who have taken a stand against the fierce, cruel and aggressive bullying and teasing that goes on every day, face to face and in cyberspace.

Thank you Elvis Presley for your music and to all the people I bugged on a nonstop basis while writing my books. And last but not least, thank you, Oprah Winfrey, for the invitation to lunch, I'll have to take a raincheck. How about next week!

Stay Tough Kids!

Mary Lee Kendal

A Pig in a Wig
By Mary Lee Kendal

Published by Masse Writers Group Naples, FL 34102
All rights reserved. No portion of this book may be reproduced in any form without permission from the publisher except as permitted by U.S copyright law.© Mary Lee Kendal

For permission contact: MaryLeeKendal (at) gmail.com

A Pig in a Wig

By Mary Lee Kendal
Illustrations by Winda Mulyasari

This book belongs to
_____

I would love to share this book with
_____